The Foodwatch Alternative Cookbook

Researched and Compiled
by
HONOR J. CAMPBELL

To Rita
For Your Better Health

Love
Lena

ASHGROVE PRESS, BATH

First published in Great Britain by
ASHGROVE PRESS LIMITED
19 Circus Place, Bath, Avon BA1 2PW

ISBN 0 906798 83 3

First published 1988

Photoset in 10½/12pt Palatino by
Ann Buchan (Typesetters), Middlesex
Printed and bound in Great Britain by
Biddles Ltd, Guildford and King's Lynn

CONTENTS

FOODWATCH INTERNATIONAL

Technical Advisory Service and Suppliers of Specialised Foods.

For further information about our service, please send an SAE to : Foodwatch International, Butts Pond Industrial Estate, Sturminster Newton, Dorset DT10 1AZ or ring Sturminster Newton (0258) 73356 between 8.30 a.m. and 5.00 p.m. on weekdays.

In this book there are many recipes where one or more of the ingredients are in themselves recipes that appear elsewhere in the book. These are denoted by an asterisk, thus (*).

FOREWORD

We started Foodwatch in 1982, with the aim of helping allergy sufferers to find foods that would suit the needs of their special diets. Many clinics and practitioners soon found our mail order service to be useful for their patients, and we have enjoyed sustained growth in all aspects of our work since its inception.

In addition to our mail order service throughout the U.K. and abroad (hence Foodwatch International) we now manufacture and supply a wide range of unique foods to retail outlets. In fact, we were the pioneers in making additive-free foods available to anyone who needed them.

Our first Cookbook was compiled to help our customers make fuller use of the specially pure foods we had available. This was followed by a second and enlarged edition, and now we have the third edition which contains many new recipes. All the recipes are free of wheat, cows' milk (apart from vegetarian cheese) and chemical additives; indeed the book is generally suitable for vegetarians and many recipes will be acceptable to vegans.

In this country we are fortunate to have such a wide variety of protein sources, vegetables and fruits available all the year round; consequently, if you are on a special diet, main meals do not seem to be so much of a problem to plan for as do breakfasts, teatimes and snacks, where many foods traditionally eaten are based on wheat and cows' milk. For this reason quite a large proportion of the recipes in this book show how cereals and carbohydrates other than wheat (and there are very many of them) can be made into appetising and nutritious dishes that are acceptable to all the family.

Some of the recipes have been submitted by our customers (who know only too well what it can be like to be really hungry on a restricted diet!), and we would like to take this opportunity to thank them for their very useful contributions.

New features of this edition include: (a) a comprehensive list of food families to help those on rotation diets, (b) detailed lists of foods showing their value in providing us with vitamins and minerals and (c) separate indexes for specific diets.

PETER AND HONOR CAMPBELL

INGREDIENTS INFORMATION

FLOURS, MEALS AND FLAKES

One of the main aims of this book is to show how the wide variety of flours, meals and flakes which we stock at Foodwatch can be used. They can be divided into various groups for dietary and culinary purposes.

Grain flours, meals and flakes. Wheat (not used in this book), rye, barley, oats, maize (corn), millet, sorghum and rice. These are made from the whole grain so contain all the goodness of the bran and germ. They are ground to varying degrees of fineness, meal being coarser than flour. This group is divided into two further groups. Those which contain *gluten* (wheat, rye, barley and oats) and those which are *gluten-free* (millet, sorghum, maize (corn) and brown rice).

Grain-free flours and flakes: Buckwheat and amaranth (which are seeds), chick pea (which is a legume), banana and chestnut. This group can be substituted for the previous group to a large extent. Soya flour is also in this group but is not interchangeable with other flours. It can be added in small amounts to recipes to give extra protein and it can be used, in some instances, as a substitute for egg.

Starchy flours: Potato, sweet potato, sago, tapioca, water chestnut, arrowroot and cornflour (cornstarch). They should be used like cornflour with which most people are familiar. They are generally interchangable with one another and are in some instances combined with flours in the other groups to give a lighter texture for breads and cakes.

PASTA

Pasta need not be ruled out for someone on a wheat-free diet. *Soba*, which is a fine spaghetti made from buckwheat, is a product of Japan. Be warned, however, that there are a number of different makes on the market and some of them do contain wheat, so read the label carefully. *Gluten-free pasta* is made from corn, rice and potato flour and is called 'Aglutella'; it is available as spaghetti or macaroni. Another useful product for adding to soups and casseroles is *Japanese Rice Noodles* which are made from rice flour, water and sea salt.

SOYA PRODUCTS

Raw soya beans contain anti-trypsin and must be fully cooked before use. Do not use them to make your own flour. Bought *Soya Flour* has been pre-cooked and is safe to use without further cooking. Soya flour can be used to replace eggs in enriched pastry and in batters and a little mixed with water can be used instead of egg for glazing pastry. *Tamari* is another soya product which is used in this book instead of soy sauce as it is wheat-free. However, as it is a fermented product, it is unsuitable for anyone on a Candida Control Diet. *Tofu*, which is sometimes called soya bean curd, comes in two types: silken tofu, which can be used to replace cream or yoghurt in desserts and sauces, and firm tofu which has a cheese-like consistency. Both are useful for anyone on a Dairy-free Diet. *Foodwatch Whole Egg Replacer* is also derived from soya beans.

SUGAR AND OTHER SWEETENERS

It appears that more people are sensitive to beet sugar than cane and that is why many of the recipes in this book suggest using *Demerara Sugar*. As this is rather coarse-grained, some of the recipes recommend that the demerara sugar be ground. This is done in a liquidiser and gives a consistency similar to caster sugar. *Maple Sugar* may be substituted for ordinary sugar in the same quantities. *Fructose*, on the other hand, is nearly twice as sweet as sugar. The *Honey* recommended for those who cannot have sugar (sucrose) is Mexican or Australian as the bees are never fed on sugar like they are in temperate zones. *Date Palm Sugar* can be substituted for sugar in recipes where the sugar is dissolved. If it is particularly hard it can be grated. Alternatives to golden syrup are *Black*

Treacle, Molasses, Clear Honey, Maple Syrup and Date Syrup.
All of these can be used in exactly the same quantities. *Sorbitol
and Dextrose (Glucose)* are not quite as sweet as sugar so a
proportionately larger amount is needed.

When substituting honey for sugar in a recipe, use honey to
the same measure recommended for sugar, but reduce the
liquid content of the recipe by one quarter. Also cook at a
slightly lower temperature. When adding honey to margarine, pour it slowly in a fine stream blending well for better
volume and texture.

EGG REPLACERS

Foodwatch Whole Egg Replacer is made from a blend of soya
proteins. It has been formulated primarily for use in cakes
where its whipping and gelling properties are used to full
advantage. It should always be folded in as the last ingredient
to ensure a good spongy texture. *Foodwatch Egg White
Replacer* is used for meringues and desserts. *Soya Flour* is
used in place of eggs to add protein in any baked goods. It can
also be mixed with a little water and used as a glaze for pastry.
Apricot and Date Egg Replacers (see recipes under section on
'Dairy Substitutes') are used where an egg would be used to
bind. Apple or pineapple purée can be used in this way too.
These are not suitable substitutes for eggs where aeration is
required.

ALTERNATIVES TO COWS' MILK

The alternatives used in this book are: goats' milk, sheep's
milk, soya milk, nut milk and coconut milk. Nutritionally
speaking all these milks make good alternatives to cows' milk,
and by using the vitamin and mineral list at the back of the
book this can be seen to be so.

Goats' Milk is the most commonly used alternative and is
usually sold frozen in 1 pint packs; it has a similar fat content
to cows' milk but the fat globules are smaller making it easier
to digest. Dried goats' milk (both whole and skimmed) are

available from Foodwatch. *Sheep's Milk* has a higher fat content than cows' and goats' milk making it highly valued for yoghurt and cheese making. Sheep's milk is also sold frozen in 1 pint packs and is becoming easier to obtain. *Soya Milk* is the most commonly used vegetable milk; it can be used as a substitute for animal milk in most applications and is widely available in both dried and liquid forms, with and without sugar. *Nut Milk* can be made from any variety of nuts, the only limitation being that if you want the milk to be white than you need to use blanched almonds or cashews. *Coconut Milk* is made either from reconstituted creamed coconut or using Coconut Milk Powder (N.B. this contains a small amount of sodium caseinate, derived from cow's milk). Recipes for nut milk and coconut milk are to be found in the section on 'Dairy Substitutes'. Both these milks are suitable for baking purposes and for serving with breakfast cereals.

Do not use any of these milks for young babies. Special formulae for babies are available on prescription from your doctor or hospital and weaning onto any of these milks for older babies should be done under the supervision of your doctor or health visitor.

CHEESE

Many people with an intolerance to milk and dairy products in general are able to eat cheese *provided* that it has been made with vegetable rennet and not calf rennet. This is why recipes using vegetable rennet cheese can be found in this book. They are available through many outlets made from goats' and sheep's milk as well as cows' milk. Also under the section on 'Dairy Substitutes' there are two recipes for *Goats' or Sheep's Curd Cheese*, one made with vegetable rennet and the other with no rennet at all. Curd cheese is very useful in cooking and can be substituted for cottage cheese or cream cheese in a wide variety of recipes.

MARGARINES, FATS AND SPREADS

Most margarines contain whey, which is a product of cows'

milk, so it is necessary for anyone on a cows' milk-free diet to change to a *Milk-free Margarine*. There are several available including Foodwatch's own brand. Milk-free margarines contain oils from differing sources and so it should be possible to find one that suits your needs. *Vegetable Fats*, of which there are a number available, are also very useful on a milk-free diet. *Foodwatch Vegetable Suet* unlike other similar products is dusted with rice flour, and *not* wheat flour, and so is gluten-free. Spreads are very useful as an alternative to margarine and are made from nuts and seeds which means they are also very nutritious. *Almond Butter, Hazelnut Butter, Peanut Butter, Sunflower Spread,* and *Tahini (Sesame Spread)* are all available sugar-free or you can make nut butters and seed spreads by following the recipes given in the section 'Dairy Substitutes' in this book.

OILS

There are a tremendous number of different kinds of edible oils to choose from and so in this book most recipes say 'oil of choice' rather than specifying a particular one. However, it needs to be said that the nutritional value of many oils is greatly reduced by cooking them. From a nutritional point of view, the best oil to use in cooking is olive as it is not harmed by heat. On the other hand it is appreciated that many who use this book will be on, or catering for those who are on, very restricted diets and rotation diets. For the highest nutritional value use cold-pressed oils, but whatever oils you use do try to make sure that they are free from antioxidants or other additives and that they are as fresh as possible.

When converting from a recipe using margarine, reduce the fat content by one third i.e. 6 oz. (170g) margarine becomes 4 fl.oz. (100 ml) oil. Oil is not suitable for use where a solid fat is melted and used as a binding agent on cooling, e.g. flapjacks.

NATURAL FLAVOURINGS

The following are suitable for flavouring cakes, desserts, sweets and drinks etc.: vanilla pods, natural vanilla flavouring, natural almond flavouring, raw cocoa powder, carob powder, 'Pionier' coffee substitute, natural fruit juice and concentrates, natural fruit flavourings, lemon juice, ground ginger, mixed spice, cinnamon, nutmeg, mace, oil of peppermint, distilled rose water, distilled orange water, rum and brandy.

The following are suitable for adding to or sprinkling on the top of breads, rolls, buns, teacakes or savoury crumbles: caraway seeds, poppy seeds, crushed sunflower seeds, sesame seeds and pumpkin seeds. Breads for serving with a savoury course may also be flavoured with herbs.

Herbs too can be used to advantage by those who cannot have stock cubes and yeast extract.

As well as adding interest to food, many of the above flavourings also add to the nutritional content.

MALIC ACID

Malic acid is the acid found in fruits such as apples and pears. It is a very good substitute for citric acid or lemon juice but must be used sparingly.

FRESH FRUIT AND VEGETABLES

There is a popular misconception that fresh fruit and vegetables will keep a long time in a refrigerator and need only be discarded when they are mouldy or, in the case of green vegetables, when they have gone yellow. This simply is not so; nutrient levels decline after fruit and vegetables have been harvested and they should be eaten as fresh as possible.

Store fresh vegetables in a plastic bag in the refrigerator. As a rough guide, watercress or mustard and cress should be used within a maximum of 24 hours and leafy vegetables such as leeks, calabrase, broccoli, spring onions and spring greens should be used within a maximum of 3 days.

It is also important for anyone who is keeping to an additive-free diet to ensure that the fruit and vegetables that they consume are organically grown whenever possible.

EGGS

Eggs, too, should be consumed when really fresh. When a hen (or bantam) goes broody she will lay an egg a day until she has a clutch, which is usually 8–12 eggs. Then she sits on them to hatch them. If she fails to sit on them for some reason, the eggs will 'go off' and by 21 days will be completely addled. Bearing this in mind, commonsense tells us that it is far better to eat eggs before 12–14 days old rather than when they are deteriorating but have not yet gone bad.

Furthermore, many people are allergic to 'Battery' eggs but not eggs from hens that are both free-range and organically fed. You have no doubt heard the phrase 'We are what we eat'; this applies to animals and birds too. In the case of hens, ordinary layers' mash can contain a colouring material to make the yolks a brighter yellow and an antibiotic to prevent disease among battery birds. However, there are a few animal feed merchants around now who can supply 'organic' layers' mash. The more demand there is for additive-free eggs the more widely available they will become. We have already seen this happen with children's drinks, so we know that such changes are possible. Also, free-range hens are sometimes fed on corn mixture (which has no colouring or antibiotic added), especially on a more old-fashioned farm where the hens run loose in the farmyard.

If you have duck, goose, bantam or quail eggs, use them by weight, bearing in mind that a standard hen's egg weighs 2 oz. without its shell.

TAP WATER

If you are having a problem trying to sort out your food sensitivites, do give a thought to your tap water. This goes into so many different foods we eat, yet in our experience many people never even consider that tap water can upset them. Yet the truth is very different, as evidence from allergy clinics shows only too well.

We can appreciate why the Water Boards add chlorine to the supply, as this kills off any bacteria present and renders the water safe to drink in this respect. However, if chlorine kills bacteria outright, what can it do to us? Remember that it was used as a poison gas during the 1914–1918 war.

Water purifiers with carbon filters will effectively remove the chlorine and most sensitive people can then drink the water without ill-effect. However nitrates and fluoride in tap water cannot be removed that easily, although it is possible at a price. Foodwatch can give you advice on all aspects of water purification.

So if you suspect your tap water, why not buy some bottles of a good spring water to start with and see if you feel better after a few days? If so, then tap water could be a problem for you.

SULPHUR DIOXIDE (SO$_2$)

This is commonly used as a preservative and can be found in many foods. Dried fruits, in particular, usually contain sulphur dioxide. If the fruits have a good colour then it is likely that they contain it. Naturally-dried fruits are much darker in colour (particularly sultanas, apricots, peaches, apples and pears). Preservatives are also usually found in the following foods unless they specifically state that they are free of preservatives: glacé cherries, candied peel, crystallised fruits, desiccated coconut, frozen fruit pulp or purée, beer, cider, wine, some fruit juices (including concentrated grape juice for home winemaking), cider vinegar, liquid pectin, golden syrup, dried vegetables, hamburgers, sausages, frozen mushrooms, powdered garlic, gelatine and jellies.

All *Foodwatch* products are guaranteed free of artificial colours, sulphur dioxide and other preservatives, and ingredients derived from cows' milk.

ARTIFICIAL COLOURS

Due to pressure to provide additive-free foods especially for children, we have seen an increasing number of food manufacturers beginning to use natural colours instead of artificial ones. However, many still do use artificial colours and it is important to read ingredients lists carefully to avoid them.

Breakfast Cereals

BUCKWHEAT PORRIDGE

Serves 2

3 oz. (*85g*) buckwheat flakes   Pinch of salt
24 fl.oz. (*700 ml*) water

Stir buckwheat flakes into water in a saucepan and add a pinch of salt. Bring to the boil. Simmer, stirring occasionally, for about 5 minutes.

To serve: Drizzle clear honey or maple syrup over the top and add goats', sheep's, soya or nut milk.

POLENTA (MAIZEMEAL PORRIDGE)

Serves 2

4½ oz. *(125g)* maizemeal   Pinch of salt
24 fl.oz. *(700 ml)* water

Blend maizemeal with a cupful of the measured water to a smooth paste. Bring rest of water to the boil in a non-stick or heavy-based saucepan. Stir in maizemeal mixture and bring back to the boil, stirring all the time until it is smooth; this prevents it sticking to the bottom of the pan. Cover and simmer very gently for 15 minutes.

To serve: Sprinkle with raw cane sugar, fructose or glucose and add goats', sheep's, soya or nut milk.

SORGHUM PORRIDGE

Serves 2

4½ oz. *(125g)* sorghum meal   Pinch of salt
24 fl.oz. *(700 ml)* water

Combine sorghum meal and water in saucepan and add salt. Bring to the boil slowly, stirring all the time. Cover and simmer gently for 15 minutes.

MILLET PORRIDGE

Serves 2

4 oz. *(110g)* millet flakes   ¾ pt. *(400 ml)* water

Combine millet flakes with water in saucepan and bring to the boil, stirring all the time until the mixture thickens. Remove from heat. Cover tightly, and stand in a warm place for 10 minutes. Add more hot water as necessary, and stir well before serving.

Variations:
(i)   Add natural raisins or chopped figs before cooking.
(ii)   Make with fruit juice instead of water.
(iii)   Make with water, goats' *or* sheep's milk and use as a substitute for mashed potatoes.

QUICK OAT PORRIDGE

Serves 2

3 oz. *(85g)* porridge oats   Pinch of salt
24 fl.oz. *(700 ml)* water

Put porridge oats and water in a saucepan, and add a pinch of salt. Bring to the boil and continue boiling for 1 minute, stirring all the time.

OATMEAL PORRIDGE

Serves 2

2 oz. (*55g*) medium oatmeal   1 pt. (*500 ml*) water

Pour the water into a saucepan and bring it to the boil. When it is boiling hard, sprinkle the oatmeal in slowly to prevent lumps forming. When the oatmeal is slightly swollen (usually 5 minutes) cover with a lid and simmer for about 30 minutes, stirring frequently. When half cooked add a pinch of salt. If salt is added earlier it will tend to harden the oatmeal.

BROWN RICE PORRIDGE

Serves 2

4½ oz. (*125g*) brown rice   1 pt. (*500 ml*) water
    flakes

Stir brown rice flakes into water in a saucepan and bring to the boil. Simmer, stirring occasionally, for 5–10 minutes.

To serve: Sprinkle with sugar or drizzle with clear honey or maple syrup and add goats', sheep's, soya or nut milk.

POPCORN

Serves 1

1 dessertspoon oil of choice   Knob of milk-free
1 dessertspoon popping   margarine
    corn (maize)   1 rounded tspn. honey

Place oil in a frying pan and heat slightly to disperse oil over the bottom of the pan. Add popping corn and immediately cover with a lid. Turn heat up to high. When you hear the first grains popping give the pan a shake. Return to heat and continue to cook until the popping stops. Remove from heat and add margarine and honey to pan to melt. Mix well and turn into a cereal bowl. Serve immediately.

APRICOT CEREAL

Serves 1

1½–2 oz. (*45–55g*) natural dried apricots

3 oz. (*85g*) porridge oats, buckwheat *or* millet flakes

Put the apricots in a basin with just enough water to cover and leave to soak overnight. Just before serving put the flakes into a cereal bowl and mix with some of the apricot liquor and then sweeten to taste if desired. Top with drained apricots.

PRUNE CEREAL

Serves 1

Follow recipe and method for 'Apricot Cereal', substituting unsorbated prunes for unsulphured dried apricots.

FRESH FRUIT CEREAL

Serves 1

1 dessert apple *or* pear   1 kiwi fruit *or* other fresh
1–2 tblspns. oat bran and   fruit in season
  oat germ

Grate the apple or pear into a cereal bowl and add sufficient
oat bran and oat germ that the mixture sticks together but is
not too dry. Decorate the top with a sliced kiwi fruit or other
fresh fruit in season. Serve immediately.

WHOLE MILLET CEREAL

1½ pts. (*750 ml*) water   2 tblspns. oil of choice
7 oz. (*200g*) whole millet   1 tspn. salt

Boil the water and then add millet, oil and salt. Bring back to
the boil, cover and simmer for 20–30 minutes until millet is
cooked and has absorbed the water.

Use for breakfast as a porridge with honey and a milk of
choice OR with a main meal instead of potato or rice.

Cold leftovers will set and can be sliced, fried and served
instead of fried bread.

WHOLE SORGHUM CEREAL

32 fl.oz. (*900 ml*) water   2 tblspns. oil of choice
6½ oz. (*185g*) whole   1 tspn. salt
    sorghum

Boil the water and then add sorghum, oil and salt. Bring back to the boil, cover and simmer for 1 hour or until sorghum is cooked and has absorbed the water.

Use for breakfast as a porridge with honey OR with a main meal instead of potato or rice. If using as part of a main meal it can be cooked in vegetable stock instead of water to give flavour.

Breads, Plain and Fancy, Scones and Teacakes

TRADITIONAL RYE BREAD

1 lb. 4 oz. (560g) rye flour
1 level tspn. salt
2 tspns. demerara sugar

3 level tspns. dried yeast *or*
1½ oz. (45g) fresh yeast
½ pt. (250 ml) water
1 tblspn. oil of choice

Place flour and salt in a bowl with 1 tspn. sugar and mix well. Put remaining sugar and yeast in lukewarm water and mix well. (If using dried yeast stand in a warm place for 10 minutes until frothy.) Add yeast liquid and oil to flour and mix to a soft dough, adding a little more liquid if necessary. Turn onto a lightly floured surface and knead well for 5 minutes. Place in an oiled polythene bag and leave to rise in a warm place until doubled in size. Reknead and divide dough into two pieces. Shape each piece and place in well oiled 1 lb. bread tins. Cover with oiled polythene and leave to rise until doubled in size again. Bake at 230°C, 450°F, Gas Mark 8 for about 40 minutes. Makes 2 loaves.

GERMAN RYE BREAD

1 lb. 8 oz. (*675g*) rye flour
1½ oz. (*45g*) fresh yeast
¾ pt. (*400 ml*) warm water
2 level tspns. salt
2 oz. (*55g*) milk-free
  margarine

2 level tspns. demerara
  sugar
50 mg tablet ascorbic acid
  (Vitamin C)
2 level tblspns. caraway
  seeds

Put 8 oz. of the flour in a mixing bowl with the sugar, yeast, crushed Vit. C tablet and warm water. Cover and leave in a warm place for 1 hour. Put the rest of the flour in a large mixing bowl with the caraway seeds and salt. Rub in the margarine. Add the yeast batter to the rubbed-in mixture and mix to make a dough. Put the dough on a lightly floured surface and knead for 10 minutes. Leave to rise in a warm place for 1 hour. Knead the risen dough again, and then shape into two rounds. Put on a greased baking sheet and make slashes in the tops with a knife. Cover and leave to rise in a warm place (preferably steamy) for about 30 minutes. Bake loaves at 180°C, 350°F, Gas Mark 4 for 45–50 minutes.
Makes 2 loaves.

RYE SODA BREAD

8 oz. (*225g*) rye flour
4 level tspns. wheat-free
  baking powder
Good pinch of salt

¼ pt. (*125 ml*) goats' *or*
  sheep's milk *or* water
1 oz. (*30g*) milk-free
  margarine *or*
1 tblspn. oil of choice

Place flour, baking powder and salt in a mixing bowl and mix well. Add other ingredients and mix to a dough. Turn out onto a lightly floured surface and knead. Form into a round loaf, cut a large cross shape on top and open it out with the side of the hand. Brush with a little milk if liked and place on a baking sheet. Bake at 230°C, 450°F, Gas Mark 8 for 15 minutes and then lower to 200°C, 400°F, Gas Mark 6 and bake for a further 10–15 minutes.

WELSH BARLEY BREAD

1 lb. 8 oz. (*675g*) barley flour
1 tspn. salt
1 tblspn. dried yeast

2 tspns. black treacle *or* honey
16 fl.oz. (*450 ml*) lukewarm water
1 tblspn. oil of choice

Put yeast and sweetener in a little extra warm water and set aside to froth. Warm flour in mixing bowl, stir in salt and then add the frothed yeast. Add the oil to the lukewarm water and mix to make a dough. Knead well and set aside to rise in a warmer place than usual i.e. the airing cupboard, for about 1½–2 hours, until doubled in size. Knock back and knead again. Place in a large but not too deep oiled or greased tin and leave to prove for up to an hour, covered and in a warm place. Make a deep cut along the top of the loaf and open it out with the side of the hand. Bake at 200°C, 400°F, Gas Mark 6 for approximately 1 hour. Sprinkle top with sesame seeds, if liked, before baking.

———

Gluten-free breads should be eaten freshly made or frozen until required as they quickly go stale. All of them make good toast and if frozen sliced may be toasted straight from the freezer.

The dough is not like wheat dough but is more like a thick batter. Some flours absorb more water than others, therefore extra water has to be added where necessary.

Most of the following recipes make 2 loaves, one to use freshly baked and the other to freeze.

POTATO AND RICE BREAD

10 oz. (*285g*) potato flour
8 oz. (*225g*) brown rice flour
½ pt. (*250 ml*) hand-hot
   water
4 tspns. dried yeast

1 tspn. sugar *or* ½ tspn.
   fructose
1 tblspn. oil of choice
½–1 tspn. salt (according to
   taste)

Put the sugar or fructose, dried yeast and hand-hot water into a jug and leave in a warm place until froth is about 1" deep. Mix flours and salt in a large bowl. Add oil and yeast mixture and mix to a thick batter adding more hand-hot water as necessary. Oil two 1 lb. loaf tins liberally and flour freely to prevent loaves sticking to tins. Divide mixture between the two tins. Leave to rise in a warm place for 20–30 minutes. (Potato flour rises well so do not leave it to rise for too long or the loaves will be full of holes.) Bake at 230°C, 450°F, Gas Mark 8 for 35–40 minutes.
Makes 2 loaves.

POTATO AND BUCKWHEAT BREAD

Follow recipe and method for 'Potato and Rice Bread' substituting the flours used in the following proportions:-

10 oz. (*285g*) potato flour   8 oz. (*225g*) buckwheat flour

POTATO AND CHESTNUT BREAD

Follow recipe and method for 'Potato and Rice Bread' substituting the flours used in the following proportions:-

12 oz. (*340g*) potato flour   6 oz. (*170g*) chestnut flour

RICE AND CHESTNUT BREAD

Follow recipe and method for 'Potato and Rice Bread' substituting the flours used in the following proportions:-

12 oz. (*340g*) brown rice flour

6 oz. (*170g*) chestnut flour

BUCKWHEAT AND RICE BREAD

Follow recipe and method for 'Potato and Rice Bread' substituting the flours used in the following proportions:-

12 oz. (*340g*) buckwheat flour

6 oz. (170g) brown rice flour

AMARANTH BREAD

Follow recipe and method for 'Potato and Rice Bread' substituting the flours used in the following proportions:-

12 oz. (*340g*) potato flour *or* brown rice flour

6 oz. (*170g*) amaranth flour

POTATO AND SOYA BREAD

4 oz. (*110g*) potato flour
4 level tblspns. soya flour
2 level tblspns. soya bran
1 tblspn. soya oil
½ oz. (*15g*) dried yeast

1 tspn. sugar
1 egg, lightly beaten
Pinch of salt
4 fl.oz. (*100 ml*) lukewarm
  water

Mix yeast with sugar, add some of the water and leave to froth. Sieve potato flour, soya flour and salt and then stir in the soya bran and oil. Mix to a thick batter with the rest of the water. Place in a tin oiled and floured with potato flour and leave to rise. Bake at 200°C, 400°F, Gas Mark 6 for 15 minutes and then turn down to 180°C, 350°F, Gas Mark 4 for a further 15–20 minutes. Turn out onto wire rack to cool.

POTATO SODA BREAD

4 oz. (*110g*) potato flour
4 level tblspns. soya flour
1–2 tblspns. soya bran
1 oz. (*30g*) milk-free
  margarine *or*
  1 tblspn. oil of choice

1 tspn. sugar (optional)
2 level tspns. wheat-free
  baking powder
1 egg, beaten
Pinch of salt
4 fl.oz. (*100 ml*) water

Sieve together potato flour, soya flour, baking powder and salt and then stir in the soya bran. Rub in margarine or oil and then add sugar. Stir again. Add beaten egg and water and whisk or beat to a smooth batter. Put into a greased or oiled and bottom-lined loaf tin and bake at 200°C, 400°F, Gas Mark 6 for about 35 minutes. Turn out onto wire rack to cool.

POTATO SODA BREAD (soya and egg-free)

8 oz. (*225g*) potato flour
8 level tblspns. any finely
  ground nuts
2 tblspns. oil of choice
4 level tspns. wheat-free
  baking powder

1 tspn. sugar (optional)
2½ fl.oz. (*62 ml*) Foodwatch
  egg white replacer
  (5% solution)
Pinch of salt
4 fl.oz. (*100 ml*) water

Put egg white replacer solution, water and salt into a bowl and whisk vigorously until it stands in stiff peaks. Sieve together potato flour and baking powder. Add to whisked solution along with rest of ingredients and beat to a smooth paste with a wooden spoon. Put into well oiled loaf tin and bake at 200°C, 400°F, Gas Mark 6 for about 35 minutes. Turn onto wire rack to cool.

Eat the same day.

MIXED FLOUR BREAD

½ oz. (*15g*) dried yeast
½ pt. (*250 ml*) lukewarm
   water
2 oz. (*55g*) milk-free
   margarine *or* 1 fl. oz.
   (*30 ml*) oil of choice
2 medium-sized eating
   apples
8½ oz. (*240g*) brown rice
   flour *or* potato flour

2 oz. (*55g*) soya flour
1 oz. (*30g*) maizemeal, millet
   or sorghum flour
1 oz. (*30g*) chick pea flour *or*
   buckwheat flour
Pinch of salt
½ oz. (*15g*) ground almonds
   or hazelnuts

Put the lukewarm water into the liquidiser goblet and sprinkle the dried yeast into it. Slice the apples, put into the liquidiser with the yeast and water and blend. Melt the margarine. Put all the dry ingredients into a large mixing bowl and add the melted margarine or oil. Stir well with a wooden spoon. Add the yeast mixture and stir very well to make a batter. Turn into 2 greased or oiled 1 lb. loaf tins and bake at 180°C, 350°F, Gas Mark 4 near the top of the oven for 40–45 minutes. Store wrapped in the fridge for up to 2 days or freeze.

The apples in this recipe greatly improve the keeping quality, however it is still a good idea to freeze the second loaf to ensure its freshness.

Makes 2 loaves.

SULTANA OR RAISIN BREAD

Add a heaped teaspoon of fructose or two heaped teaspoons
of sugar to the above recipe along with 2 oz. (55g) natural
sultanas or raisins before the final mixing.

CHICK PEA BREAD

18 oz. (505g) chick pea flour	1 tspn. sugar
18 fl.oz. (500 ml) hand-hot water	2 oz. (55g) milk-free margarine
4 tspn. dried yeast	1 tspn. salt

Put the sugar or fructose, dried yeast and hand-hot water into
a jug and leave in a warm place until froth is about 1" deep.
Mix flour and salt in a large bowl. Add margarine and rub in to
the flour. Add yeast mixture and mix to a thick batter adding
more hand-hot water, if necessary. Grease two 1 lb. loaf tins
liberally and flour freely with chick pea flour to prevent loaves
sticking to the tins. Divide mixture between the two tins.
Leave to rise in a warm place for 20–30 minutes.
Bake at 230°C, 450°F, Gas Mark 8 for 35–40 minutes.
Makes 2 loaves.

MILLET BREAD

4 oz. (*110g*) millet flour
1 medium-sized carrot,
    grated
1 tblspn. clear honey
1 tspn. salt

2 tblspns. cold water
8 fl.oz. (*200 ml*) boiling water
2 tblspns. oil of choice
2 eggs

Combine the millet flour, carrot, honey, salt and oil in a bowl. Mix well. Stir in boiling water. Separate the eggs, beat the yolks well and add 2 tblspns. (*30 ml*) cold water and continue to beat. Add to flour mixture. Fold in stiffly beaten egg whites. Shape the dough and place on an oiled baking tray. Bake at 180°C, 350°F, Gas Mark 4 for about 40 minutes.

SORGHUM BREAD

Follow the recipe and method for 'Millet Bread' substituting sieved sorghum meal for millet flour. The coarser particles which are removed from the sorghum meal can be used for Sorghum Porridge.

RICE, SOYA AND RAISIN BREAD

6 oz. (*170g*) brown rice flour
2 oz. (*55g*) soya flour
4 tblspns. soya milk
2 eggs
4 tblspns. soya oil

4 tblspns. sugar *or* honey
2 tspns. wheat-free
    baking powder
2 oz. (*55g*) natural raisins
1 oz. (*30g*) chopped nuts

Mix milk, eggs, honey and oil. Sieve dry ingredients and gradually blend into the mixture. Stir in the raisins and nuts. Pour into a well-oiled bread tin and leave to rest for 1 hour. Bake at 180°C, 350°F, Gas Mark 4 for 45 minutes.

MALT LOAF

4 level tblspns. malt extract
4 level tblspns. maple syrup
1½ oz. (*45g*) milk-free
  margarine
8 oz. (*225g*) barley flour
4 level tspns. wheat-free
  baking powder

Pinch of salt
4 oz. (*110g*) natural raisins
1 egg *or* ½ oz. (*15g*)
  Foodwatch Whole Egg
  Replacer and 3 tblspns.
  water
6 tblspns. goats' *or* sheep's
  milk

Grease and bottom line a 2 lb. loaf tin. Measure maple syrup and malt extract carefully, levelling off spoon with a knife. Place in a saucepan together with the margarine and melt over gentle heat.

If using egg:-   Put egg in a bowl with the milk and whisk. Place dry ingredients in a large bowl and stir in raisins. Make a 'well' in the centre and add all the rest of the ingredients at the same time. Beat well with a wooden spoon until smooth.

If using whole egg replacer:-   Put whole egg replacer in a small basin with the 3 tblspns. (*45 ml*) water and whisk with a rotary beater until fluffy. Place the dry ingredients in a large bowl and stir in the raisins. Make a 'well' in the centre and pour in the malt mixture and the milk. Beat well with a wooden spoon until smooth. Fold in the whipped whole egg replacer.

Put mixture into prepared tin and level off the top. Bake in centre of oven at 160°C, 325°F, Gas Mark 3 for 1–1¼ hours. Test with a knife or skewer to make sure centre is completely cooked. After removing from oven leave in the tin for 5–10 minutes and then turn out onto a wire rack until cold. Store in an airtight tin. The flavour develops on keeping.

DATE AND WALNUT LOAF

3 oz. (*85g*) potato flour
3 oz. (*85g*) buckwheat flour
3 level tspns. wheat-free
baking powder
A pinch of salt
½ level tspn. bicarbonate of
soda
1½ oz. (*45g*) muscovado
sugar
2 oz. (*55g*) dates, chopped

1½ oz. (*45g*) walnuts,
chopped
1½ oz. (*45g*) black treacle
¾ oz. (*25g*) milk-free
margarine
¼ pt. (*125ml*) goats', sheep's
or soya milk
½ oz. (*15g*) Foodwatch
Whole Egg Replacer
3 tblspns. water

Grease and line a 1 lb. loaf tin. Sieve the flours, baking powder, salt and bicarbonate of soda into a mixing bowl. Stir in the muscovado sugar, chopped dates and walnuts. Warm the measured treacle, margarine and milk together until the margarine melts. Put 3 tblspns. (*45 ml*) water into a small mixing bowl, add the whole egg replacer and whisk until fluffy. Stir the warmed liquid into the flours and then gradually fold in the whisked whole egg replacer. Pour into prepared tin and bake at 180°C, 350°F, Gas Mark 4 for 1–1¼ hours or until well risen and firm. Turn onto a cooling rack, remove paper and leave until quite cold. Serve sliced and spread with milk-free margarine.

MILLET FRUIT LOAF

½ oz. (*15g*) dried yeast
½ pt. (*250 ml*) boiling water
4 oz. (*110g*) natural sultanas
or raisins
8 oz. (*225g*) millet flour

3 oz. (*85g*) potato flour
2 oz. (*55g*) soya flour
2 fl.oz. (*50 ml*) oil of choice

Soak dried fruit in ½ pt. (*250 ml*) boiling water for 15 minutes. Liquidise and then check for temperature. Re-heat to blood-heat if necessary. Stir in yeast and leave for about 10 minutes until frothy. Put flours together in a large mixing bowl and add yeast mixture and oil. Mix well with a wooden spoon and pour into 2 oiled 1 lb. loaf tins. Bake at 180°C, 350°F, Gas Mark 4 for 40–45 minutes.
Makes 2 loaves.

MAIZEMEAL BREAD

8 oz. (*225g*) maizemeal
4 level tspns. wheat-free
   baking powder
½ tspn. salt

½ pt. (*250 ml*) goats', sheep's
  or soya milk
3 tblspns. corn oil
1 egg

Brush an 8″ or 9″ tin with corn oil. Blend or whisk all ingredients together well. Pour into prepared tin. Bake at 220°C, 425°F, Gas Mark 7 for 20–25 minutes or until golden brown. Cut into squares while still in the tin and then transfer to a wire rack to cool.

MILLET BATTER BREAD

Follow recipe and method for 'Maizemeal Bread' substituting millet flour for maizemeal.

BROWN RICE BATTER BREAD

Follow recipe and method for 'Maizemeal Bread' substituting brown rice flour for maizemeal.

BANANA BATTER BREAD

Follow recipe and method for 'Maizemeal Bread' substituting banana flour for maizemeal.

SORGHUM BATTER BREAD

Follow recipe and method for 'Maizemeal Bread' substituting sieved sorghum meal for maizemeal. (The coarse particles which are removed from the sorghum meal by sieving can be used for Sorghum Porridge.)

BARLEY SCONES

8 oz. (*225g*) barley flour
4 level tspns. wheat-free
   baking powder
2 oz. (*55g*) milk-free
   margarine *or* 2 tblspns.
   oil of choice

1 oz. (*30g*) sugar *or* ½ oz.
   (*15g*) fructose
5 fl.oz. (*125 ml*) goats',
   sheep's *or* soya milk *or*
   water

Sieve flour and baking powder into a bowl. Rub in the margarine or oil, then add sugar or fructose. Add milk or water all at once, and mix to a soft dough. Turn onto a floured surface and knead dough quickly until smooth. Roll out to about ½" thickness and cut into 2" rounds. Transfer to a greased or oiled baking tray. Brush tops with milk of choice, if liked. Bake at top of oven at 230°C, 450°F, Gas Mark 8 for 7–10 minutes.

Makes approx. 10 scones.

RYE SCONES

Follow the recipe and method for 'Barley Scones' substituting rye flour for barley flour.

SAGO SCONES

8 oz. (225g) sago flour
4 level tspns. wheat-free
  baking powder
2 oz. (55g) milk-free
  margarine *or*
  2 tblspns. oil of choice

1 oz. (30g) sugar *or* ½ oz.
  (15g) fructose
4 fl.oz. (100 ml) goats',
  sheep's *or* soya milk *or*
  water

Sieve flour and baking powder into a bowl. Rub in the margarine or oil, then add sugar or fructose. Add milk or water all at once, and mix to a soft dough. Turn onto a floured surface and knead dough quickly until smooth. Roll out to about ½" thickness and cut into 2" rounds. Transfer to a greased or oiled baking tray. Bake at top of oven at 230°C, 450°F, Gas Mark 8 for 7–10 minutes. Cool on wire rack.

Makes approx. 10 scones.

Eat same day.

BANANA SCONES

8 oz. (225g) banana flour
4 level tspns. wheat-free
  baking powder
2 tblspns. oil of choice

1 oz. (30g) demerara sugar
Up to 6 fl.oz. (150 ml) goats',
  sheep's *or* soya milk *or*
  water

Put the dry ingredients into a bowl and stir in the oil. Work in the liquid until sufficient has been added to form a stiff but pliable dough. Roll out on banana flour and cut into rounds with a 2½" cutter. Put on a baking tray and bake at 230°C, 450°F, Gas Mark 8 for 10 minutes. Eat while still hot.

CHICK PEA SCONES

9 oz. (*255g*) chick pea flour
4 level tspns. wheat-free
  baking powder
2 oz. (*55g*) milk-free
  margarine

1 oz. (*30g*) sugar *or* ½ oz.
  (*15g*) fructose
5 fl.oz. (*125 ml*) water

Sieve flour and baking powder into a bowl. Rub in margarine and then add sugar or fructose. Add water all at once and mix to a soft dough. Turn onto a well-floured surface and knead, using extra flour as necessary, until smooth. Roll out to about ½" thickness and cut into 2" rounds. Transfer to a baking tray and bake at the top of the oven at 230°C, 450°F, Gas Mark 8 for 10 minutes. Cool on wire rack.

Makes 10 scones.

Eat same day, preferably whilst still hot.

CHESTNUT AND POTATO SCONES

5 oz. (*140g*) potato flour
4 oz. (*110g*) chestnut flour
4 level tspns. wheat-free
  baking powder

2 oz. (*55g*) milk-free
  margarine
1 oz. (*30g*) sugar *or* ½ oz.
  (*15g*) fructose
5 fl.oz. (*125 ml*) water

Sieve flours and baking powder into a bowl. Rub in margarine and stir in oil, then add sugar or fructose. Add water all at once and mix to a soft dough. Turn onto a well-floured surface and knead using more flour if necessary until smooth. Roll out to about ½" thickness and cut into 2" rounds. Transfer to a greased baking tray and bake at top of oven at 230°C, 450°F, Gas Mark 8 for 7–10 minutes. Cool on a wire rack.

Makes approx. 10 scones.

BUCKWHEAT AND POTATO SCONES

Follow the recipe and method for 'Chestnut and Potato Scones' substituting buckwheat flour for chestnut flour.

BUCKWHEAT SCONES

8 oz. (*225g*) buckwheat
  flakes
½ level tspn. bicarbonate of
  soda
2½ fl.oz. (*65 ml*) nut milk*

1 tblspn. sunflower oil
½ oz. (*15g*) maple sugar

Grind the buckwheat flakes in a liquidiser. Mix the bicarbonate of soda with the nut milk. Put all the ingredients into a bowl and mix well. Roll into 8 balls with the palms of the hands and place them on a baking sheet. Flatten the tops and bake at 230°C, 450°F, Gas Mark 8 for 10 minutes.

TEA CAKES

6 oz. (*170g*) chick pea flour
6 oz. (*170g*) potato flour
2 oz. (*55g*) arrowroot flour
1 oz. (*30g*) buckwheat flour
1 oz. (*30g*) chestnut flour
5 level tspns. wheat-free
    baking powder

5 oz. (*140g*) natural currants
3 oz. (*85g*) natural sultanas
2 oz. (*55g*) cashews *or*
    almonds
5 fl.oz. (*125 ml*) cold water
1 tblspn. honey
7 fl.oz. (*200 ml*) hot water

Sieve flours and baking powder into a large mixing bowl. Stir in the dired fruit. Put nuts and cold water into liquidiser and blend until smooth. Dissolve honey in hot water and add both liquids to the flours and mix well. Can be cooked in individual Yorkshire pudding tins or sandwich tins, according to the size of the tea cakes required. Oil the tins and dust with sieved chick pea flour. Pour the mixture into the tins and smooth sides and top with the back of a spoon. Bake at 200°C, 400°F, Gas Mark 6 for about 25 minutes. Can be eaten immediately or frozen when cold and toasted straight from the freezer.

MILLET AND FRUIT SLICE

½ oz. (*15g*) dried yeast
½ pt. (*250 ml*) boiling water
5 oz. (*140g*) natural currants
4 fl.oz. (*100 ml*) oil of choice

12 oz. (*340g*) millet flour
5 oz. (*140g*) barley *or* brown
    rice flour
2 oz. (*55g*) soya flour

Chop currants finely and soak in the boiling water for 15 minutes. Check for temperature and re-heat to blood-heat if necessary. Stir in yeast and leave for about 10 minutes until frothy.
Stir in oil and flours to make a stiff dough. Roll out thinly and cut into squares.
Arrange on oiled baking sheets and let stand for 15 minutes. Bake at 130°C, 250°F, Gas Mark ½ for 40 minutes or until light gold in colour.

MILLET AND RICE KNOBS

4 oz. (*110g*) millet flour
3½ oz. (*90g*) brown rice flour
½ oz. (*15g*) ground almonds
  or cashews
4 level tspns. wheat-free
  baking powder

2 oz. (*55g*) vegetable suet
  with rice flour
Pinch of salt
5 fl.oz. (*125 ml*) goats',
  sheep's *or* soya milk

Sieve flours and baking powder into a bowl. Stir in ground nuts, salt and finally vegetable suet. Mix to a soft dough with the milk. Put dessertspoonfuls into greased or oiled bun tins and bake at 230°C, 450°F, Gas Mark 8 for 10 minutes. Cool on wire rack and serve instead of bread or scones.

CHICK PEA MUFFINS

10 oz. (*285g*) chick pea flour
2 oz. (*55g*) maple sugar
7 fl.oz. (*200 ml*) nut milk*
3 level tspns. wheat-free
  baking powder

Pinch of salt
2 tblspns. oil of choice
2 oz. (*55g*) natural sultanas
  or raisins
4 tblspns. apricot *or* date egg
  replacer*

Oil 12 muffin cups or bun tins. Put all the dry ingredients into a bowl. Add the rest of the ingredients and mix well. Put the mixture into the prepared tins and bake at 220°C, 425°F, Gas Mark 7 for 15 minutes.

Waffles, Drop Scones and Pancakes

All the recipes in this section are cooked either on a griddle or in a frying pan or waffle maker.

WAFFLES
(with egg)

Waffles are an ideal food for the whole family and are invaluable for anyone on a yeast-free diet. They can be made from a wide variety of ingredients and they are both appetizing and nutritious.

Any of the following flours, meals or flakes will make good waffles: brown rice flour, millet flour, chick pea flour, chestnut flour, banana flour, rye flour, barley flour, sorghum meal, oatmeal, porridge oats, buckwheat flakes or millet flakes.

6 oz. (*170g*) flour, meal *or*
   flakes of choice (see
   above)
2 level tspns. wheat-free
   baking powder
Pinch of salt

1 level tblspn. sugar
   (optional)
1 tblspn. oil of choice
5 10 fl.oz. (*125 250 ml*)
   goats', sheep's, soya,
   nut* *or* coconut milk*
1 egg

Put all ingredients, except the milk, into a bowl. Add 5 fl.oz. (*125 ml*) milk and beat well, adding more liquid as necessary until the batter is thick and smooth. (The amount of liquid will vary with the type of cereal used.) Leave to stand while the waffle iron is heating up. Adjust the consistency with more liquid, if necessary, as the mixture will thicken as it stands. Use an electric waffle maker or standard waffle iron which fits over hotplate. Brush liberally with oil all surfaces which will come into contact with the waffles. Use approx. 1½ tblspns. batter for each waffle. Cook for 3–4 minutes if using an electric waffle maker. For a standard waffle iron, adjust cooking time accordingly. Waffles freeze well and can be reheated under the grill or in an electric toaster. Serve them for breakfast instead of toast, for hot snacks or at teatime. These serving suggestions are in addition to the traditional way of serving waffles with ice cream or a sweet sauce for dessert.

SOYA WAFFLES (egg-free)

Follow the recipe and method for 'Waffles' (with egg) substituting 3 heaped tblspns. soya flour for the egg and using soya oil and soya milk.

EGG-FREE WAFFLES

Follow the recipe and method for 'Waffles' (with egg) substituting 2 tblspns. Apricot Egg Replacer*, Date Egg Replacer* or pineapple purée for the egg. The sugar may be replaced with maple syrup or date syrup if desired.

DROP SCONES

Drop Scones or Griddle Scones as they are sometimes called are made on a hot griddle or a lightly oiled frying pan.

The batter used is exactly the same as that used for Waffles. Drop tablespoonfuls onto a hot griddle or frying pan and cook for about three minutes on each side or until golden brown. Serve hot.

CHEESE DROP SCONES

Add 3 oz. (*85g*) grated vegetable rennet cheese to the batter but do not add any sugar.

WALNUT AND HONEY DROP SCONES

These make a special treat for teatime. Add 2 oz. (*55g*) finely chopped walnuts to the batter and sweeten with 1 tblspn. honey instead of sugar.

PANCAKES

Pancakes are made with a thinner batter than waffles and drop scones.

Use the same recipe as for waffles but increase the amount of liquid so that the batter flows easily and when poured into the frying pan will quickly coat the base of the pan. Cook until golden brown and then turn and brown the other side. Serve hot with a savoury or sweet filling.

WHOLE SORGHUM DROP SCONES

7 oz. (*200g*) whole sorghum
2 egg whites

2 tblspns. water
A good pinch of salt

Wash the whole sorghum to remove any dust, place in a bowl and cover with water. Leave to soak overnight. Drain off liquid. Put the soaked and drained cereal into a liquidiser and blend to a smooth paste.
Whisk egg whites with 2 tblspns. water and then stir in the liquidised sorghum to make a thin batter.
Drop by spoonfuls onto an oiled and heated frying pan. Brown well on both sides. Serve spread with nut butter or sunflower seed spread, yeast extract or honey.

WHOLE MILLET DROP SCONES

Follow recipe and method for 'Whole Sorghum Drop Scones' substituting whole millet for whole sorghum.

SWEET POTATO PANCAKE

3 oz. (*85g*) sweet potato flour   1 apple *or* pear
1 oz. (*30g*) milk-free
    margarine

Mix sweet potato flour and milk-free margarine together in mixing bowl. Add chopped or grated fruit. Mix together well and roll out. Heat a knob of margarine in frying pan. Place pancake into pan and cook gently and evenly on medium heat until golden brown, then turn and brown other side.

MILLET CHAPATTI

4½ oz. (*125g*) millet flakes   1 tspn. salt
4 fl.oz. (*100 ml*) water

Mix ingredients in a bowl and knead well. Break off small portions and roll in little balls. Roll balls out flat and thin between the palms of the hands or with a rolling pin. Cook in an oiled heavy-based frying pan. Chapatti is cooked when brown spots appear.
Makes 5–6 chapatti.

POTATO GRIDDLE SCONES

1 lb. (*450g*) mashed potato   A little potato flour
1 egg, beaten   A little oil of choice

Add beaten egg and a little oil to the mashed potato. Mix well and then mix in a little potato flour to stiffen the mixture. Form into round cakes with the hands and cook on a hot griddle or frying pan until golden brown on each side.
Serve hot.

Biscuits, Savoury and Sweet

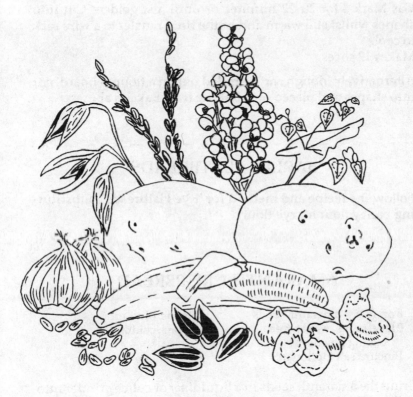

RYE FLATBREADS

8 oz. (225g) rye flour
2 level tspns. wheat-free
   baking powder
3 oz. (85g) milk-free
   margarine *or* 2 fl.oz.
   (50 ml) oil of choice

Pinch of salt
4 tblspns. water

Place fat or oil, water and half of the flour in a bowl and cream together. Sieve baking powder and salt with the rest of the flour, add to the mixture and work to a soft dough. Work to fit into a Swiss Roll tin. Flatten top with a rolling pin. Prick or mark in furrows with a fork, if desired. Bake at 180°C, 350°F, Gas Mark 4 for 20–22 minutes or until just golden. Cut into shapes whilst still warm and in the tin. Transfer to a wire rack to cool.
Makes 12 slices.

Alternatively, dough can be rolled out on a floured board, cut into shapes and placed on a baking tray. Bake as above.

BARLEY FLATBREADS

Follow the recipe and method for 'Rye Flatbreads', substituting barley flour for rye flour.

AMARANTH CRISPBREAD

8 oz. (225g) amaranth seeds
2 level tspns. wheat-free
   baking powder
Pinch of salt (optional)

3 tblspns. olive oil
4 tblspns. cold water

Grind the amaranth seeds in a liquidiser or coffee grinder into as fine a flour as possible. Stir in the baking powder and salt. Add the oil and mix well. Finally, add the water and mix until well blended. Tip the mixture into a Swiss Roll tin and, using a fork, press the mixture into place until it is evenly distributed over the tin. Flatten well and make furrows with the fork. Mark out 12 crispbread shapes with a knife. Bake at 180°C, 350°F, Gas Mark 4 for 20 minutes. Cool slightly and then carefully remove crispbreads with a palette knife and place on a wire rack until completely cold.
Makes 12 slices.

RICE AND BUCKWHEAT CRISPBREAD

6 oz. (*170g*) brown rice flour
2 oz. (*55g*) buckwheat flour

2 tblspns. milk-free
    margarine *or* oil of choice
Water to mix

Mix all ingredients together using just enough water to make a dough. Roll out thinly on a surface dusted with flour. Cut into oblong biscuits and bake at 220°C, 425°F, Gas Mark 7 for 8–10 minutes.

TAPIOCA CRISPBREAD

8 oz. (*225g*) tapioca flour
2 level tspns. wheat-free
    baking powder
Pinch of salt

4 oz. (*110g*) milk-free
    margarine *or*
    vegetable fat
3 tblspns. water

Place margarine or fat, water and salt together with one third of the flour in a mixing bowl and cream with a fork until just mixed. Sieve remaining flour and baking powder together and add to the mixture. Knead very thoroughly until smooth. Roll out the dough thinly on a lightly floured surface. Cut into squares and place on a greased baking sheet. Bake at 180°C, 350°F, Gas Mark 4 for approx. 25 minutes.

SAGO CRISPBREAD

9 oz. (*255g*) sago flour
2 level tspns. wheat-free
    baking powder
Pinch of salt

4 oz. (*110g*) milk-free
    margarine *or*
    vegetable fat
3 tblspns. water

Follow method and baking instructions for 'Tapioca Crispbread'.

ARROWROOT CRISPBREAD

Follow the recipe and method for 'Tapioca Crispbread', substituting arrowroot flour for tapioca flour.

SCOTTISH OATCAKES

8 oz. (225g) medium oatmeal
Pinch of bicarbonate of soda
6 tblspns. boiling water

1 tblspn. oil of choice
Pinch of salt (optional)

Place oatmeal in a large mixing bowl and stir sieved bicarbonate of soda very well to ensure even distribution. Make a well in the centre of the oatmeal. Add the boiling water and the oil to the oatmeal and mix well to a stiff dough. Roll out thinly on a surface dusted with oatmeal. Cut into rounds using a plain cutter or upturned cup. Place on a greased baking tray and bake at 180°C, 350°F, Gas Mark 4 for 25 minutes. Do not allow to brown.

BREAKFAST BISCUITS

4 oz. (110g) barley flour
1½ oz. (45g) potato flour
½ oz. (15g) medium oatmeal
¼ level tspn. salt
½ level tspn. wheat-free
    baking powder

1½ oz. (45g) milk-free
    margarine
1½ oz. (45g) demerara sugar,
    ground or ¾ oz. (22g)
    fructose
3 tblspns. goats', sheep's or
    soya milk

Sieve together flour, salt and baking powder into a large bowl and add the oatmeal. Rub in margarine, then add sugar or fructose. Mix to a stiff paste with milk. Turn out onto a lightly barley-floured surface and knead well. Roll out thinly and cut into rounds with a 2" or 2½" biscuit cutter. Transfer to a greased baking tray and prick well. Bake at 190°C, 375°F, Gas Mark 5 for 15–20 minutes or until light brown. Transfer to wire rack to cool. Store in an airtight tin. Serve with marmalade as an alternative to toast.

BUCKWHEAT BREAKFAST BISCUITS

3 oz. (*85g*) milk-free
  margarine
6oz. (*170g*) buckwheat flour
2 oz. (*55g*) sago flour

2 level tspns. wheat-free
  baking powder
Pinch of salt
4 tblspns. water

Put fat, water and half the buckwheat flour in a bowl and cream together. Sieve salt and baking powder with the rest of the flours, add to the mixture and work to a soft dough. Roll out on a surface dusted with buckwheat flour and cut out with a 2½" round biscuit cutter. Prick all over with a fork. Place on a baking tray and bake at 180°C, 350°F, Gas Mark 4 for 20 minutes. Put on a wire rack to cool and store in an airtight tin. Serve as crispbreads.

CHESTNUT BISCUITS

Follow the recipe and method for 'Buckwheat Breakfast Biscuits', substituting chestnut flour for buckwheat flour.

BARLEY AND WALNUT COOKIES

2½ oz. (*70g*) milk-free
  margarine
2 oz. (*55g*) demerara sugar,
  ground *or* 1¼ oz. (*36g*)
  fructose
2 oz. (*55g*) walnuts, finely
  chopped

4 oz. (*110g*) barley flour
2 level tspns. 'Pionier'
  coffee substitute
1 tblspn. water

Cream margarine and sugar or fructose until light and fluffy, and add walnuts. Stir in sieved flour and 'Pionier'. Take heaped teaspoonfuls of the mixture and roll into balls. Place onto a greased baking tray, spacing well apart, and flatten with the palm or a potato masher. Bake at 190°C, 375°F, Gas Mark 5 for 15–20 minutes. Allow to cool slightly on baking tray and then transfer to a wire rack until cold. Store in an airtight tin.

RYE DIGESTIVE BISCUITS

3½ oz. (*100g*) rye flour
¼ level tspn. salt
½ level tspn. wheat-free
  baking powder
1½ oz. (*45g*) milk-free
  margarine

½ oz. (*15g*) medium oatmeal
1 oz. (*30g*) sugar *or* ½ oz.
  (*15g*) fructose
3 tblspns. goats', sheep's *or*
  soya milk

Sieve together flour, salt and baking powder into a large bowl, and add oatmeal. Rub in margarine and add sugar or fructose. Mix to a stiff paste with milk. Turn onto a surface lightly dusted with rye flour. Knead well and roll out thinly. Cut into rounds with a 2½" biscuit cutter. Transfer to a greased baking tray and prick well. Bake at 190°C, 375°F, Gas Mark 5 for 12–15 minutes. Transfer to wire rack to cool. Store in an airtight tin.

BROWN RICE DIGESTIVE BISCUITS

4 oz. (*110g*) brown rice flour
¼ level tspn. salt
½ level tspn. wheat-free
   baking powder

1½ oz. (*45g*) milk-free
   margarine
1 oz. (*30g*) sugar *or* ½ oz.
   (*15g*) fructose
3 tblspns. goats', sheep's *or*
   soya milk

Follow method and baking instructions for 'Rye Digestive Biscuits'.

TEA-TIME BISCUITS

3 oz. (*85g*) chick pea flour *or*
   barley flour
2 oz. (*55g*) brown rice flour
   or potato flour
1 oz. (*30g*) soya flour

2 oz. (*55g*) milk-free
   margarine
2 oz. (*55g*) sugar *or* 1 oz.
   (*30g*) fructose
2–4 tspns. water

Put flours and margarine into a bowl and rub in well. Stir in sugar or fructose and add water, a little at a time, to form a dough. Knead until the mixture is smooth and then roll out with a little extra flour. Cut into rounds with a pastry cutter or upturned cup, transfer to a baking tray and prick all over with a fork. Bake at 160°C, 325°F, Gas Mark 3 for 10–12 minutes. Carefully remove biscuits from tray while still warm and leave on a wire rack to cool. Store in an airtight tin.

GINGER NUTS

2½ oz. (*70g*) milk-free
  margarine
3 oz. (*85g*) demerara sugar *or*
  maple sugar
3 oz. (*85g*) clear honey *or*
  maple syrup
8 oz. (*225g*) brown rice flour
  or chick pea flour

½ level tspn. mixed spice
1½ level tspns. ground
  ginger
1 level tspn. bicarbonate of
  soda
1 tblspn. warm water

Put margarine, sugar and honey or syrup into a pan and melt over very low heat. Sieve flour, spice and ginger into a large bowl. Add melted mixture and bicarbonate of soda mixed with warm water. Mix well and shape into approximately 24 small balls. Put onto greased baking trays, well apart to allow them to spread. Flatten tops with a potato masher. Bake at 160°C, 325°F, Gas Mark 3 for 15 minutes. Leave on trays for 1 or 2 minutes to set before transferring to a wire rack to cool. Store in an airtight tin.

FRUITY OAT BISCUITS

5 oz. (*140g*) oatmeal
½ tspn. bicarbonate of soda
Pinch of salt

1½ tblspns. oil of choice
1–2 tblspns. fruit purée
4 fl.oz. (*100 ml*) water

Grind the oatmeal to a fine flour in a liquidiser. Put a couple of tablespoonsful of the flour into a mixing bowl, add the salt, oil and some of the fruit purée and mix well. Stir the bicarbonate of soda into the rest of the flour and then rub the two mixtures together, adding more fruit purée as necessary, until the mixture resembles breadcrumbs. Add the water and make a soft dough. Form into 8 balls, place on an oiled baking tray and flatten tops with a potato masher. Bake at 230°C, 450°F, Gas Mark 8 for 15–20 minutes.

ARROWROOT AND COCONUT BISCUITS

4 oz. (*110g*) desiccated
coconut (preservative-
free)
4 oz. (*110g*) arrowroot flour
2 level tspns. wheat-free
baking powder

2 oz. (*55g*) milk-free
margarine
1 oz. (*30g*) fructose
2 dessertspns. water to mix

Put all dry ingredients into a mixing bowl. Rub in the margarine and then add the water. Knead to a soft dough. Roll out on a surface dusted with arrowroot flour and cut out with a fluted biscuit cutter. Bake at 180°C, 350°F, Gas Mark 4 for 12–15 minutes or until light golden in colour. Leave on tray to partially cool before transferring to a wire rack.

BUCKWHEAT FLAPJACKS

3 oz. (*85g*) milk-free
margarine
3 oz. (*85g*) demerara sugar
1 dessertspn. black treacle

4 oz. (*110g*) buckwheat
flakes
Pinch of salt

Melt margarine, sugar and treacle in a saucepan (do not allow it to boil.) Add buckwheat flakes and stir well. Put into a shallow oblong tin and bake at 180°C, 350°F, Gas Mark 4 for 20–22 minutes. After removing from the oven leave to set for a few minutes. Cut into fingers while still warm and transfer to a wire rack until completely cold.

BUCKWHEAT AND WALNUT BISCUITS

4 oz. (*110g*) buckwheat   1 egg, beaten
  flakes   2 oz. (*55g*) walnuts, ground
2 tblspns. muscovado sugar
4 tblspns. oil of choice

Mix buckwheat flakes, sugar, ground walnuts, oil and beaten egg in a bowl. Transfer mixture to an oiled oblong tin (9" x 7"). Smooth top with back of a spoon. Bake at 180°C, 350°F, Gas Mark 4 for 20–22 minutes. Cut into squares and cool on wire rack.

MILLET AND HAZELNUT BISCUITS

4 oz. (*110g*) millet flakes   1 egg, beaten
2 tblspns. muscovado sugar   2 oz. (*55g*) hazelnuts,
4 tblspns. oil of choice   ground

Mix millet flakes, sugar, ground hazelnuts, oil and beaten egg in a bowl. Transfer mixture to an oiled oblong tin (9" x 7"). Smooth top with back of a spoon. Bake at 180°C, 350°F, Gas Mark 4 for 20–22 minutes. Cut into squares and cool on wire rack.

ALMOND PYRAMIDS

2 oz. (*55g*) ground almonds   2 tblspns. clear honey *or*
3 oz. (*85g*) potato flour *or*   maple syrup
  brown rice flour   1 egg, beaten
2 oz. (*55g*) milk-free   Pinch of salt
  margarine

Beat the margarine and honey or syrup to a cream. Add the ground almonds, flour and salt. Add the beaten egg and mix to a stiff paste. Place in small mounds on an oiled baking sheet and shape into pyramids with a fork. Bake at 180°C, 350°F, Gas Mark 4 for about 20 minutes.

BANANA COOKIES

3 oz. (*85g*) milk-free
  margarine
2 oz. (*55g*) demerara sugar
2 oz. (*55g*) chopped dried
  banana

4 oz. (*110g*) banana flour
3 tblspns. goats', sheep's *or*
  soya milk

Put all ingredients into a mixing bowl and beat well. The dough should be very stiff. Roll out on a banana floured surface and cut into biscuits OR put onto a baking tray in little heaps using a teaspoon. Bake at 180°C, 350°F, Gas Mark 4 for 15–20 minutes.

Makes 12–14 cookies.

CHOCOLATE OR CAROB RICE BISCUITS

4 oz. (*110g*) milk-free
  margarine
4 oz. (*110g*) sugar *or* 2 oz.
  (*55g*) fructose
1 egg, beaten

9 oz. (*255g*) brown rice flour
1 oz. (*30g*) pure cocoa
  powder *or* carob powder

Cream together margarine and sugar or fructose until light and fluffy. Beat in egg gradually. Sieve together flour and cocoa or carob and stir into mixture. Knead lightly on a surface dusted with brown rice flour. Roll out thinly and cut into rounds with a 2" or 2½" biscuit cutter. Place on a greased baking tray, leaving room to spread and bake at 160°C, 325°F, Gas Mark 3 for about 20 minutes. Allow to cool slightly before transferring to a wire rack to cool completely. Sandwich together in pairs with Chocolate or Carob Filling*.

BUCKWHEAT FLAKE BISCUITS

6 oz. (*170g*) milk-free
    margarine
1 tspn. maple syrup
4 oz. (*110g*) sugar
5 oz. (*140g*) buckwheat flour

1½ level tspns. wheat-free
    baking powder
4 oz. (*110g*) buckwheat
    flakes
1 tspn. bicarbonate of soda
1 tblspn. boiling water

Melt the margarine and syrup in a pan over gentle heat. Stir in the sugar, sifted flour and baking powder followed by the flakes. Mix together the bicarbonate of soda and the boiling water. Stir into the biscuit mixture. Place small heaps of the mixture well apart on a greased baking tray and bake at 180°C, 350°F, Gas Mark 4 for 12–15 minutes or until golden brown.

BUCKWHEAT FINGERS

8 oz. (*225g*) buckwheat
    flakes
Pinch of salt
5 oz. (*140g*) milk-free
    margarine
1 level tblspn. honey *or*
    maple syrup

2 oz. (*55g*) demerara sugar *or*
    maple sugar
2 oz. (*55g*) dates, finely
    chopped
Pinch of ground ginger

Put margarine, sugar and honey or syrup into a saucepan and set over a low heat until the margarine has melted. Stir in all other ingredients and mix well. Pour into a greased 7" square tin and bake at 190°C, 375°F, Gas Mark 5 for approx. 30 minutes. Cool slightly, then cut into fingers whilst still in tin. Turn out when cold.

MILLET FINGERS

Follow the recipe and method for 'Buckwheat Fingers' substituting millet flakes for buckwheat flakes.

GLUTEN-FREE FLORENTINES

3 oz. (*85g*) milk-free
   margarine
4 oz. (*110g*) demerara sugar
4 oz. (*110g*) chopped
   walnuts

2 oz. (*55g*) flaked hazelnuts
   or almonds
2 oz. (*55g*) natural sultanas
   or raisins
1 tblspn. brown rice flour

Melt the margarine and sugar together in a saucepan over gentle heat. Add the remaining ingredients all at once and stir well to mix. Line baking sheets with non-stick paper and drop in mounds, using a spoon, spacing well apart on the prepared sheets. Press into neat shapes. Bake at 180°C, 350°F, Gas Mark 4 for 12–15 minutes, until golden. Leave on paper until cold and then remove carefully. Coat with Carob Icing*.

POTATO SHORTBREAD

6 oz. (*170g*) potato flour
4 oz. (*110g*) milk-free
   margarine

2 oz. (*55g*) sugar
3 oz. (*85g*) almonds *or*
   cashews, ground

Beat margarine until soft and creamy. Add other ingredients and work until a ball of dough is formed. Put into a greased 7" or 8" round sandwich tin and press down evenly. Prick all over and bake at 180°C, 350°F, Gas Mark 4 for 35–40 minutes or until lightly golden brown. Cut into 8 wedges.

RICE SHORTBREAD

6 oz. (*170g*) brown rice flour   2 oz. (*55g*) sugar
4 oz. (*110g*) milk-free
   margarine

Cream margarine and sugar and then work in the flour. Knead until the mixture forms a ball of dough and leaves the sides of the bowl clean. Press evenly into a 7" or 8" sandwich tin and prick all over. Bake at 160°C, 325°F, Gas Mark 3 for 40 minutes or until lightly golden. Allow to cool a little in the tin and then cut into 8 wedges. Transfer to a wire rack until cold.

SWEET POTATO SHORTBREAD

Follow recipe and method for 'Rice Shortbread' substituting sweet potato flour for brown rice flour. (A little raw cocoa powder or carob powder may be added with the flour to flavour.)

TAPIOCA SHORTBREAD

5 oz. (*140g*) tapioca flour   2 oz. (*55g*) sugar
4 oz. (*110g*) milk-free
   margarine

Cream all ingredients together and then work until it forms a ball of dough and leaves the sides of the bowl clean. Put into a greased 7" or 8" sandwich tin and press down evenly. Prick all over and bake at 160°C, 325°F, Gas Mark 3 for 50 minutes. Allow to cool in tin a little and then cut into 8 wedges. Transfer to a wire rack until cold.

SAGO SHORTBREAD

8 oz. (*225g*) sago flour   2 oz. (*55g*) sugar
4 oz. (*110g*) milk-free
    margarine

Follow the method and baking instructions for 'Tapioca Shortbread' using an 8" or 9" tin.

Cakes, Fillings and Frostings

TAPIOCA VIENNESE FANCIES

4 oz. (*110g*) tapioca flour
4 oz. (*110g*) milk-free
  margarine

2 oz. (*55g*) sugar
A little jam

Beat all ingredients except jam together until creamy. Transfer mixture to a piping bag fitted with a large star nozzle. Pipe into paper cake cases in a bun tin. Start with a little mixture in the centre at the bottom and then pipe two rows in a spiral to leave a hollow in the middle. Bake at 160°C, 325°F, Gas Mark 3 for 50 minutes. Cool on wire rack. When completely cold fill the centres with jam. May be dusted with icing sugar, if desired. Makes 6–7 cakes.

COCONUT ROCKS

5 tblspns. potato flour
2 tblspns. milk-free
  margarine
3 tblspns. desiccated
  coconut (preservative-
  free)

3 tblspns. clear honey *or*
  maple syrup
1 egg, beaten

Beat the margarine together with the honey or syrup. Add the flour and coconut gradually, then the egg, still beating the mixture. Drop from a teaspoon onto an oiled baking tray and bake at 220°C, 425°F, Gas Mark 7 for about 8 minutes.

COCONUT MACAROONS

2 egg whites
4 oz. (*110g*) demerara sugar,
  ground *or* caster sugar

3½ oz. (*100g*) desiccated
  coconut (preservative-
  free)

Whisk the egg whites very stiffly, then fold in the sugar and coconut and mix well. Line a baking sheet with rice paper and drop dessertspoonfuls onto the rice paper, well apart to allow them to spread. Bake at 150°C, 300°F, Gas Mark 2 for 20–25 minutes. Remove from tray and peel off excess rice paper.

Makes 8–10 macaroons.

BELGIAN BISCUIT CAKE

1 oz. (*30g*) milk-free
   margarine
1 tblspn. golden syrup *or*
   maple syrup
2¼ oz. (*60g*) Bournville Plain
   chocolate *or* Plamil Carob
   Bar

4 oz. (*110g*) Sweet Biscuits*
   or Shortbread*
1 oz. (*30g*) natural sultanas
½ oz. (*15g*) stem ginger,
   finely chopped
Rum *or* orange liqueur
   (optional)

Any of the plain sweet biscuits or shortbreads mentioned in this book would be suitable for this recipe.

Place the biscuits in a plastic bag and crush with a rolling pin. Put margarine, syrup and chocolate or carob in a pan and melt VERY gently. Add the crumbs and the rest of the ingredients and then stir well until the crumbs are completely coated with the mixture. A little rum or orange liqueur may be added, if desired. Pat into a small tin and leave to set. Store in the refrigerator until required. Cut into small wedges and serve as an after-dinner treat.

COCONUT RICE FINGERS (sugar-free)

6 oz. (*170g*) brown rice flour
½ oz. (*15g*) sesame seeds
1½ oz. (*45g*) desiccated
   coconut (preservative-
   free)
4 level tspns. wheat-free
   baking powder

Pinch of salt
½ pt. (*250 ml*) goats', sheep's
   or soya milk
3 tblspns. oil of choice
1 egg *or* ½ oz. (*15g*) Foodwatch whole egg replacer
   + 3 tblspns. water

If using egg:-
Put all ingredients together into a large bowl and whisk well.

If using whole egg replacer:-
Put the egg replacer and water into a bowl and whisk until frothy. Put rest of ingredients into a separate bowl, add 2 tablespoonsful of the whisked egg replacer and mix well. Fold in the rest of the whisked egg replacer.

Pour the prepared mixture into an oiled Swiss Roll tin and bake at 220°C, 425°F, Gas Mark 7 for 15–20 minutes.
Allow to cool in the tin and then cut into fingers. Transfer to a wire rack until completely cold.

RYE SPONGE CAKES

4 oz. (*110g*) rye flour
4 oz. (*110g*) sugar
2 tblspns. water
1½ level tspns. wheat-free baking powder

4 oz. (*110g*) milk-free margarine *or* 2½ fl.oz. (*65 ml*) oil of choice
2 eggs, beaten

Cream margarine and sugar together. Add beaten eggs. Sieve flour and baking powder together and fold into mixture together with the water to make a sponge batter. Put dessertspoonfuls of the mixture into paper cake cases on a baking tray and bake at 200°C, 400°F, Gas Mark 6 for 12–15 minutes.

This recipe can be adapted for many different kinds of cakes and sponge puddings. For suggestions see rice flour sponge recipes.

MILLET OR SORGHUM ROCK CAKES

3 oz. (*85g*) millet *or* sorghum flour
3 oz. (*85g*) brown rice flour *or* chick pea flour
2 oz. (*55g*) milk-free margarine
1 egg
1 tspn. wheat-free baking powder

3 oz. (*85g*) sugar *or* 1½ oz. (*45g*) fructose
1 oz. (*30g*) natural currants
Pinch of each nutmeg and mixed spice
Goats', sheep's *or* soya milk to mix

Mix flours and baking powder together. Rub in milk-free margarine and add sugar, spice and currants. Mix well. Add egg and a little milk and mix to a very stiff dough. Place in mounds on a greased baking sheet and bake at 200°C, 400°F, Gas Mark 6 for 15 minutes.

CHEWY COCONUT BARS

First Layer:-
4 oz. (*110g*) flour of choice
3 oz. (*85g*) milk-free margarine
3 oz. (*85g*) demerara sugar, ground

Second Layer:-
2 eggs, slightly beaten
½ tspn. salt

Pinch of vanilla powder
3 oz. (*85g*) desiccated coconut (preservative-free)
3 oz. (*85g*) chopped walnuts
1 oz. (*30g*) flour of choice
6 oz. (*170g*) demerara sugar, ground

Beat margarine and sugar together until fluffy and mix in flour. Put mixture into a greased 13" x 9" x 2" cake tin and bake for 10 minutes at 180°C, 350°F, Gas Mark 4.

Put all ingredients for second layer into a bowl and mix well. Spread mixture over first layer. Return to the oven and bake for a further 20 minutes. Cool. Cut into bars and leave in tin until completely cold.

COCONUT BROWNIES

2 oz. (*55g*) Bournville Plain Chocolate *or* Plamil Chocolate *or* Plamil Carob Bar
2½ oz. (*70g*) milk-free margarine
2 eggs
6 oz. (*170g*) sugar

3 oz. (*85g*) brown rice flour *or* banana flour
½ tspn. wheat-free baking powder
¼ tspn. salt
2½ oz. (*70g*) desiccated coconut (preservative-free)

Topping:
½ oz. (*15g*) milk-free
   margarine
1 tblspn. demerara sugar
2½ oz. (*70g*) desiccated
   coconut (preservative-
   free)

Melt chocolate or carob and milk-free margarine in a bowl over a pan of hot water. Set aside to cool. Beat eggs until fluffy. Gradually add sugar and beat until well blended. Add melted chocolate or carob, flour, baking powder, salt and coconut. Beat well and spread into a greased 8" square tin.

To make the topping:-
Melt the margarine and stir in the rest of the sugar and coconut. Scatter evenly over the cake batter and bake for 30 minutes at 180°C, 350°F, Gas Mark 4. Cool in tin and cut into 16 squares. Transfer to wire rack until completely cold.

RICE AND SULTANA BUNS

4 oz. (*110g*) brown rice flour
4 oz. (*110g*) sugar *or* 4½ oz.
   (*125g*) glucose *or* 2½ oz.
   (*70g*) fructose
2 tblspns. water
4 oz. (*110g*) milk-free
   margarine *or* 2½ fl.oz.
   (*65 ml*) oil of choice

2 eggs, beaten
1½ level tspns. wheat-free
   baking powder
3 oz. (*85g*) natural sultanas

Sieve flour and baking powder together. Add all the rest of the ingredients except the sultanas and beat very well. Stir in sultanas. Put dessertspoonfuls into paper cake cases on a baking tray and bake at 200°C, 400°F, Gas Mark 6 for approx. 15 minutes.

Variations:
Natural raisins, chopped dates or figs may be used instead of
sultanas.

MILLET BUNS

4 oz. (*110g*) milk-free
    margarine
4 oz. (*110g*) sugar
2 eggs, beaten

4 oz. (*110g*) millet flour
4 oz. (*110g*) natural currants
1 oz. (*30g*) flaked almonds *or*
    hazelnuts

Cream margarine and sugar until light and fluffy. Fold in
beaten eggs and millet flour a little at a time and finally stir in
the fruit and nuts. Put dessertspoonfuls into paper cake cases
on a baking tray or into greased bun tins. Bake at 200°C, 400°F,
Gas Mark 6 for 15–20 minutes.

POTATO AND BUCKWHEAT BUNS

2 oz. (*55g*) potato flour
2 oz. (*55g*) buckwheat flakes
4 oz. (*110g*) sugar *or* 4½ oz.
    (*125g*) glucose *or* 2½ oz.
    (*70g*) fructose
2 tblspns. water

4 oz. (*110g*) milk-free
    margarine *or* 2½ fl.oz.
    (*65 ml*) oil of choice
2 eggs, beaten
1½ level tspns. wheat-free
    baking powder

Sieve potato flour and baking powder together and stir in
buckwheat flakes. Put all ingredients into a mixing bowl and
beat very well with a wooden spoon. Put dessertspoonfuls
into paper cake cases on a baking tray or into greased bun
tins. Bake at 200°C, 400°F, Gas Mark 6 for approx. 15 minutes.

EGGLESS SPONGE CAKES

6 oz. (*170g*) brown rice flour
1½ level tspns. wheat-free
   baking powder
4 oz. (*110g*) milk-free
   margarine

4 oz. (*110g*) sugar *or* 2 oz.
   (*55g*) fructose
1 oz. (*30g*) Foodwatch
   egg replacer
6 tblspns. water

Cream margarine and sugar or fructose until pale and fluffy. Put whole egg replacer and water into a bowl and whisk well. Sieve flour and baking powder together, and gently fold flour and a little whisked egg replacer into creamed mixture. Finally fold in the rest of the whisked egg replacer. Put into paper cake cases and bake at 200°C, 400°F, Gas Mark 6 for 15–20 minutes.

EGGLESS ROCK CAKES

8 oz. (*225g*) brown rice flour
5 oz. (*140g*) milk-free
   margarine
2½ level tspns. wheat-free
   baking powder
5 oz. (*140g*) sugar *or* 2½ oz.
   (*70g*) fructose

2 oz. (*55g*) natural raisins
2 oz. (*55g*) natural sultanas
2 oz. (*55g*) natural currants
½ oz. (*15g*) Foodwatch
   whole egg replacer
3 tblspns. water

Sieve flour and baking powder together into a large mixing bowl. Put whole egg replacer and water into a bowl and whisk well. Rub margarine into flour and stir in sugar or fructose. Fold in egg replacer mixture to make a stiff consistency. Gently stir in dried fruit. Put mixture into paper cake cases or greased bun tins and bake at 220°C, 425°F, Gas Mark 7 for about 10–12 minutes.

MUD HUTS

Chocolate or Carob Sponge Cakes with Chocolate or Carob Filling. These little cakes were a childhood favourite named by my brother when he was very small.

4 oz. (*110g*) milk-free
   margarine *or* 2½ fl.oz.
   (*65 ml*) oil of choice
4 oz. (*110g*) sugar *or* 4½ oz.
   (*125g*) glucose *or* 2½ oz.
   (*70g*) fructose
2 eggs, beaten

4 oz. (*110g*) brown rice flour
1 level tspn. raw cocoa
   powder *or* carob powder
1½ level tspns. wheat-free
   baking powder
2 tblspns. water
A little jam (optional)

If using margarine: Put margarine and sweetener into a large bowl and cream together until fluffy. Add beaten egg. Sieve together flour, baking powder and cocoa or carob. Beat into creamed mixture together with water.

If using oil: Sieve together flour, baking powder and cocoa or carob into a large bowl. Add all the rest of the ingredients and beat very well.

Put dessertspoonfuls into paper cake cases on a baking tray or into greased bun tins and bake at 200°C, 400°F, Gas Mark 6 for approx. 15 minutes. Put on a wire rack to cool. Cut a small lid out of the top of each cake. Put a tiny blob of jam in each hollow (optional). Cover jam with a tspn. of Chocolate or Carob Filling* and replace the lid.

Makes 12 cakes.

APRICOT SQUARES (egg-free)

4 oz. (*110g*) natural dried
   apricots
¼ pt. (*125 ml*) water
4 oz. (*110g*) porridge oats,
   buckwheat flakes *or*

millet flakes
4 oz. (*110g*) potato flour *or*
   tapioca flour
1½ level tspns. wheat-free
   baking powder

2 oz. (*55g*) sugar *or* maple
  sugar
4 oz. (*110g*) milk-free

margarine
2 level tblspns. honey,
  maple *or* golden syrup

Grease a shallow 7" square tin with milk-free margarine. Place apricots in a pan with the water. Bring to the boil and then simmer gently, stirring occasionally, until all the water has been absorbed and apricots are tender. Beat mixture until smooth.

Sieve flour and baking powder into a bowl and stir in flakes and sugar. Rub in margarine until mixture begins to stick together. Measure honey or syrup carefully and blend into cake mixture. Press half of the cake mixture into base of tin, spread apricots over this and then top with remaining cake mixture. Spread evenly. Bake at 190°C, 375°F, Gas Mark 5 for 35–40 minutes, until cake is golden brown. Leave to become quite cold in the tin, cut into squares and remove from tin.

DATE SQUARES

Follow recipe and method for 'Apricot Squares' substituting dates for apricots. Date syrup may also be substituted for honey, maple or golden syrup.

BUCKWHEAT CRUNCHY TOPPED SQUARES

Topping:
2 oz. (*55g*) natural sultanas *or* raisins
3 oz. (*85g*) milk-free margarine
1 rounded tblspn. golden *or* maple syrup
3 oz. (*85g*) buckwheat flakes
3 oz. (*85g*) desiccated coconut (preservative-free)
2 oz. (*55g*) demerara sugar

Cake:
4 oz. (*110g*) milk-free margarine
4 oz. (*110g*) demerara sugar, ground
2 oz. (*55g*) potato flour
2 oz. (*55g*) buckwheat flour
1½ level tspns. wheat-free baking powder
2 eggs *or* 1 oz. (*30g*) Foodwatch whole egg replacer and 6 tblspns. water

For topping: Put the margarine and syrup into a saucepan and set over gentle heat until margarine has melted. Stir in rest of ingredients and set aside.

For cake with egg: Cream the margarine and sugar until fluffy. Beat the eggs and add with the rest of the ingredients and mix well.

For cake with whole egg replacer: Cream the margarine and sugar until fluffy. Put the whole egg replacer into a large bowl together with the 6 tblspns. water and whisk well. Put the dry ingredients into the creamed mixture together with a spoonful of the whisked egg replacer and mix well. Fold in the rest of the whisked egg replacer.

Spread cake mixture over the base of a greased and lined 9" x 7" (approx.) tin, cover with the topping and smooth top with the back of a spoon. Bake at 180°C, 350°F, Gas Mark 4 for 50 minutes or until golden brown.

Makes 12 squares.

MILLET CRUNCHY TOPPED SQUARES

Topping:
2 oz. (*55g*) natural sultanas *or* raisins
3 oz. (*85g*) milk-free margarine
1 rounded tblspn. golden *or* maple syrup
3 oz. (*85g*) millet flakes
3 oz. (*85g*) desiccated coconut (preservative-free)
2 oz. (*55g*) demerara sugar

Cake:
4 oz. (*110g*) milk-free margarine
4 oz. (*110g*) demerara sugar, ground
4 oz. (*110g*) millet flour *or* brown rice flour
1½ level tspns. wheat-free baking powder
2 eggs *or* 1 oz. (*30g*) Foodwatch whole egg replacer and 6 tblspns. water

For topping: Put the margarine and syrup into a saucepan and set over gentle heat until margarine has melted. Stir in rest of ingredients and set aside.

For cake with egg: Cream the margarine and sugar until fluffy. Beat the eggs and add with the rest of the ingredients and mix well.

For cake with whole egg replacer: Cream the margarine and sugar until fluffy. Put the whole egg replacer into a large bowl together with the 6 tblspns. water and whisk well. Put the dry ingredients into the creamed mixture together with a spoonful of the whisked egg replacer and mix well. Fold in the rest of the whisked egg replacer.

Spread cake mixture over the base of a greased and lined 9" x 7" (approx.) tin, cover with the topping and smooth top with the back of a spoon. Bake at 180°C, 350°F, Gas Mark 4 for 50 minutes or until golden brown.

Makes 12 squares.

GLUTEN-FREE FRUIT CAKE

9 oz. (*255g*) chick pea flour
1 rounded tblspn. wheat-
  free baking powder
1 level tspn. cinnamon
1 level tspn. mixed spice
3 level tblspns. milk-free
  margarine

12 fl.oz. (*340 ml*) water
2 medium-sized eating
  apples
1 medium-sized carrot
5 oz. (*140g*) natural currants
5 oz. (*140g*) natural sultanas

Sieve flour, baking powder and spices together into a large bowl. Chop apple and carrot, put into liquidiser with the measured water and blend. Add to flour mixture along with other ingredients and beat well with a wooden spoon. Pour mixture into a greased 8″ cake tin and bake in centre of the oven at 190°C, 375°F, Gas Mark 5 for approximately 1 hour. Eat within one week.

Note: Do not line the cake tin with paper as it will stick to the cake.

TROPICANA CAKE

4 oz. (*110g*) milk-free
  margarine
2 tspns. lemon rind, grated
11 oz. (*310g*) banana flour
2 level tspns. wheat-free
  baking powder
1½ oz. (*45g*) toasted
  desiccated coconut
  (preservative-free)

4 fl.oz. (*100 ml*) pineapple
  juice
3 oz. (*85g*) demerara sugar *or*
  maple sugar
2 eggs *or* 1 oz. (*30g*)
  Foodwatch whole egg
  replacer + 6 tblspns.
  water
3 dried bananas, chopped

Cream margarine and sugar, add lemon rind and beat well. Add eggs one at a time, beating well after each addition. Sieve together flour and baking powder. Fold into mixture alternately with pineapple juice and toasted coconut. Add chopped dried bananas and mix well. Put mixture into a greased and bottom-lined 2 lb. loaf tin and bake at 180°C, 350°F, Gas Mark 4 for 1–1¼ hours.

If using whole egg replacer: Whisk the whole egg replacer with the water and fold into the cake mixture as the final ingredient.

FUDGE CAKE

2 oz. (*55g*) Plamil Plain Chocolate *or* Plamil Carob Bar *or* Bournville Plain Cocolate
2 tblspns. water
4 oz. (*110g*) milk-free margarine
7 oz. (*200g*) soft brown sugar
Pinch of natural vanilla
2 eggs
¼ pt. (*125 ml*) goats', sheep's *or* soya milk
Juice of ½ lemon
7 oz. (*200g*) brown rice flour *or* banana flour
½ level tspn. wheat-free baking powder
1 level tspn. bicarbonate of soda
2 tblspns. apricot jam, warmed

Frosting:
1 lb. (*450g*) demerara sugar
½ pt. (*125 ml*) water
1 good tblspn. (*20 ml*) golden *or* maple syrup
2 oz. (*55g*) milk-free margarine
1½–2 oz. (*45–55g*) raw cocoa powder *or* carob powder

Line a 7" round cake tin with greased greaseproof paper.

Break chocolate or carob bar into small pieces in bowl. Add the water and stand over a pan of gently boiling water stirring occasionally until smooth; remove from heat and allow to cool slightly. Cream the margarine with sugar and vanilla until light and fluffy. Beat in lightly whisked eggs and melted chocolate or carob. Add the lemon juice to the milk. Sieve together the flour, baking powder, and bicarbonate of soda. Add these two mixtures, a little at a time and alternately, to the cake mixture, beating after each addition. Turn mixture into prepared tin and smooth over the top. Bake at 180°C, 350°F, Gas Mark 4 for 1–1½ hours or until cake is cooked through. Leave to cool in tin for 10 minutes before turning on to a wire rack. When cold brush the sides of cake with jam and then spread fudge frosting over the top, using a palette knife to swirl the frosting.

To prepare Fudge Frosting:
Place sugar, water, syrup, 2 oz. milk-free margarine and cocoa *or* carob into heavy-based pan. Stir over gentle heat until sugar has dissolved. Bring to 234°F on a sugar thermometer, then remove from heat. Cool for 10–15 minutes, then beat with wooden spoon until thick and spreading consistency. Use at once.

RICE FLOUR SPONGE CAKE

4 oz. (*110g*) brown rice flour
4 oz. (*110g*) sugar *or* 4½ oz. (*125g*) glucose *or* 2½ oz. (*70g*) fructose
2 tblspns. water

4 oz. (*110g*) milk-free margarine *or* 2½ fl.oz. (*65 ml*) oil of choice
2 eggs, beaten
1½ level tspns. wheat-free baking powder

If using margarine: Cream margarine and sweetener of choice, and then add eggs. Sieve together flour and baking powder and fold into mixture with water.

If using oil: Sieve flour and baking powder together. Add all the rest of the ingredients and beat very well.

Put into a greased and brown rice-floured 7" or 8" sandwich tin and bake at 200°C, 400°F, Gas Mark 6 for 20–22 minutes. Remove from oven and allow to stand for a few minutes and then turn out onto a wire rack to cool.

CRUNCHY TOPPING FOR RICE CAKE

1 egg white
3 oz. (*85g*) sugar

1 oz. (*30g*) ground almonds
or hazelnuts
1 oz. (*30g*) desiccated
coconut (preservative-
free)

Whisk egg white till stiff and standing in peaks. Carefully fold in the other ingredients. Spread over the cake mixture and bake in the usual way.

RICH CHOCOLATE/CAROB CAKE

For Rich Mocha Cake add the optional ingredients.

3 eggs
4 oz. (*110g*) castor sugar
1 oz. (*30g*) brown rice flour
¼ tspn. wheat-free baking
powder
1 oz. (*30g*) raw cocoa powder
or carob powder
1 tspn. instant chicory *or*
coffee (optional)

Icing and decoration:
4 oz. (*110g*) milk-free
margarine
6 oz. (*170g*) icing sugar
½ level tspn. raw cocoa
powder, carob powder,
instant coffee *or* instant
chicory
2 oz. (*55g*) Bournville Plain
Chocolate *or* Plamil
Chocolate *or* Plamil
Carob Bar

Grease and line two 9″ sandwich tins with greased greaseproof paper. Break the eggs into a mixing bowl over a pan of hot water, add the sugar and whisk for about 8 minutes till thick. Remove the bowl from the heat and continue to whisk till the mixture is cool. Sift the flour, baking powder, cocoa or carob and the instant chicory or coffee, if using, and fold into the mixture. Divide evenly between the two prepared tins. Bake in the centre of oven at 190°C, 375°F, Gas Mark 5 for about 20 minutes till cooked. Cool in the tins for 5 minutes and then carefully turn out on to a cooling tray.

To ice and decorate: Cream the margarine, gradually beating in the icing sugar which has been sieved with the flavouring of choice. Continue beating until smooth. Stand one cake on the serving plate and spread with half the icing and place second cake on top. Spread remaining icing over the top and rough up the surface with the palette knife. Coarsely grate the chocolate or carob bar over the top and dredge with icing sugar.

COCONUT CAKE

5½ oz. (*155g*) milk-free
    margarine
8 oz. (*225g*) demerara sugar,
    ground
4 eggs
8 oz. (*225g*) brown rice flour
    or banana flour

3 level tspns. wheat-free
    baking powder
4 oz. (*110g*) desiccated
    coconut (preservative-
    free)
3 tblspns. goats', sheep's or
    soya milk

Grease and line an 8", deep cake tin. Cream together the margarine and sugar until fluffy. Beat the eggs lightly and gradually beat into creamed mixture, alternately with the flour and baking powder. Finally add the coconut and the milk. Put into the prepared tin and smooth over the top. Bake at 160°C, 325°F, Gas Mark 3 for 1½ hours.

HONEY AND HAZELNUT CAKE

6 oz. (*170g*) brown rice flour
    or barley flour
Pinch of salt
½ tspn. mixed spice
1 oz. (*30g*) milk-free
    margarine
⅓ pt. (*165 ml*) clear honey

1 egg
¾ tspn. bicarbonate of soda
3 tblspns. goats', sheep's *or*
    soya milk
3 tblspns. flaked hazelnuts

Put the honey and margarine in a small pan over low heat until margarine is melted. Remove from the heat and mix. Sieve together the flour, salt, and spices. Add these to the melted mixture with the egg and beat well. Dissolve the bicarb. in the milk and stir into cake mixture. Turn into a greased and floured sandwich tin and sprinkle with the flaked hazelnuts. Bake at 180°C, 350°F, Gas Mark 4 for 25–30 minutes. Turn out onto a wire rack to cool.

BANANA FLOUR SPONGE CAKE

4 oz. (*110g*) banana flour
1½ level tspns. wheat-free
    baking powder
4 oz. (*110g*) milk-free
    margarine

4 oz. (*110g*) demerara sugar
2 eggs
2 tblspns. water

Grease a 7" or 8" sandwich tin and line the bottom with greaseproof paper.
Place all ingredients together in a mixing bowl and beat very well until light and fluffy. Put into prepared tin and bake at 200°C, 400°F, Gas Mark 6 for 20 minutes.

OATEN FRUIT LOAF

2 level tblspns. organic
    porridge oats
4 oz. (*110g*) demerara sugar
4 oz. (*110g*) organic porridge
    oats
1 level tspn. wheat-free
    baking powder
4 oz. (*110g*) natural raisins

4 oz. (*110g*) natural sultanas
4 oz. (*110g*) natural dried
    apricots, chopped
2 oz. (*55g*) hazelnuts,
    chopped *or* flaked
2 oz. (*55g*) almonds, nibbed
    or flaked
3 eggs

Grease and line the bottom of a 2 lb loaf tin with greaseproof paper. Sprinkle the sides of the tin with the 2 level tblspns. porridge oats. Beat the sugar and eggs until creamy. Add 4 oz. oats and baking powder, mixing well. Stir in the chopped fruit and nuts, press into the tin and level the surface. Bake at 180°C, 350°F, Gas Mark 4 for 1½ hours, covering the top with greaseproof paper if it gets too brown. Cool on a wire rack. Make a week before required and store in an airtight tin.

WALNUT CAKE

6 oz. (*170g*) milk-free margarine

6 oz. (*170g*) demerara sugar, ground *or* 3¾ oz. (*105g*) fructose

1 level tblspn. instant chicory, coffee *or* Pionier coffee substitute

2 oz. (*55g*) shelled walnuts, chopped

8 oz. (*225g*) barley flour

3 level tspns. wheat-free baking powder

3 eggs and 1 tblspn. water *or* 1½ oz. (*45g*) Foodwatch whole egg replacer and 8 fl.oz. (*200 ml*) water

Cream margarine and sugar or fructose until light and fluffy.

If using eggs: Beat eggs and add a little at a time, beating well after each addition. Add water and beat again. Then fold in sieved dry ingredients and chopped walnuts.

If using whole egg replacer: Put whole egg replacer in a large bowl. Add 8 fl.oz. (*200 ml*) water and whisk well. Sieve dry ingredients and fold both mixtures into creamed margarine a little at a time until well mixed. Add chopped walnuts and stir gently into cake mixture. Place mixture in a greased 2 lb. loaf tin with a piece of greaseproof paper in the base. Level top with the back of a spoon and bake at 160°C, 325°F, Gas Mark 3 for 1¼–1½ hours. Leave to cool in tin for about 10 minutes before turning out onto a wire rack to cool completely. Cut cake in half and spread with Fructose Cream Filling* or Vanilla Cream Filling* and then sandwich back together again.

BARLEY PARKIN

6 oz. (*170g*) barley flakes
6 oz. (*170g*) black treacle
3 oz. (*85g*) milk-free
   margarine *or* 2 fl.oz.
   (*50 ml*) oil
2 tblspns. goats', sheep's *or*
   soya milk
½ level tspn. bicarbonate of
   soda

3 oz. (*85g*) muscovado sugar
2 oz. (*55g*) barley flour
2 level tspns. ground ginger
1 egg *or* ½ oz. (*15g*)
   Foodwatch whole egg
   replacer + 3 tblspns.
   water

Mince the barley flakes. Sieve the flour, bicarbonate of soda and ginger. Stir in the barley flakes, sugar and beaten egg. Warm the milk-free margarine (if using) and the treacle and stir into the mixture. Beat in the oil (if using). Beat well and pour into greased or oiled and bottom-lined 8″ x 8″ tin and bake for about 40 minutes at 180°C, 350°F, Gas Mark 4. Keep for a few days before use to allow the cake to mature.

If using whole egg replacer: Whisk the whole egg replacer with the water and fold into the cake mixture as the last ingredient.

PARKIN (egg-free)

8 oz. (*225g*) barley flour
Pinch of salt
2 level tspns. wheat-free
   baking powder
2 level tspns. ground ginger
4 oz. (*110g*) milk-free
   margarine

8 oz. (*225g*) medium oatmeal
4 oz. (*110g*) demerara sugar,
   ground
8 oz. (*225g*) black treacle
3 fl.oz. (*75 ml*) pure apple
   juice
3 fl.oz. (*75 ml*) water

Sieve flour, salt, baking powder and ground ginger into a bowl. Rub in margarine, then stir in oatmeal and sugar. Warm treacle, then pour treacle, apple juice and water into centre of dry ingredients. Beat lightly until thoroughly blended. Turn into greased and lined 9" square tin. Bake at 180°C, 350°F, Gas Mark 4 for 40–50 minutes. Leave to cool in tin for 10 minutes before transferring to a wire rack. Make a week or so before required and store in an airtight tin.

GINGERBREAD

4 oz. (*110g*) milk-free margarine *or* 2½ fl.oz. (*65 ml*) oil of choice
4 oz. (*110g*) black treacle
½ pt. (*250 ml*) goats', sheep's *or* soya milk
10 oz. (*285g*) brown rice flour
3½ level tspns. wheat-free baking powder

1 tspn. ground ginger
½ tspn. mixed spice
Pinch of salt
8 oz. (*225g*) demerara sugar, ground
1 egg, beaten *or* ½ oz. (*15g*) Foodwatch whole egg replacer and 3 tblspns. water
1 level tspn. bicarbonate of soda

If using egg: Place margarine (if using), treacle and all except 4 tblspns. of the milk in a pan. Set over gentle heat and melt but do not boil. Sieve flour, baking powder, ginger, mixed spice and salt into a bowl. Stir in the sugar. Pour melted ingredients into a well in centre of the flour. Add the oil (if using), beaten egg and the bicarbonate of soda which has been dissolved in the reserved 4 tblspns. of milk. Beat well until smooth.

If using whole egg replacer: Place margarine (if using), treacle and all except 4 tblspns. of the milk in a pan. Set over gentle heat and melt but do not boil. Sieve flour, baking powder, ginger, mixed spice and salt into a bowl. Stir in the sugar. Pour melted ingredients into a well in centre of the flour. Add the oil (if using) and the bicarbonate of soda which has been dissolved in the reserved 4 tblspns of milk. Beat well until smooth. Put the whole egg replacer into a large bowl. Add 3 tblspns. water and whisk well. Fold the whisked whole egg replacer into the cake mixture.

Pour into a greased and lined 8" or 9" square tin. Bake at 180°C, 350°F, Gas Mark 4 for ½ hour, then reduce heat to 160°C, 325°F, Gas Mark 3 for a further ¾ hour. Cover with a sheet of greaseproof paper during the later stages of baking to prevent the top from burning. Best made a few days before required and stored in an airtight tin.

HONEY TEA LOAF (sugar-free)

3 oz. (*85g*) natural raisins
3 oz. (*85g*) natural sultanas
¼ pt. (*125 ml*) cold rooibosch tea
4 tblspns. clear honey

2 tblspns. water
1 egg, beaten
8 oz. (*225g*) brown rice flour
3 level tspns. wheat-free baking powder
Honey to glaze

Put fruit into a basin and cover with cold rooibosch tea. Leave to soak overnight. Stir in egg and beat well. Sieve together flour and baking powder. Add to mixture and mix thoroughly. Turn into a greased and lined 1 lb. loaf tin and bake at 180°C, 350°F, Gas Mark 4 for 1–1¼ hours until firm and browned. Leave to cool in tin for 10 minutes, then turn onto a wire rack until cold. Brush top with honey to give a sticky glaze.

This loaf will improve in flavour and become more moist if stored in an airtight tin for a few days before use.

Variations: Instead of brown rice flour use:
(i) 4 oz. (*110g*) sago flour and 4 oz. (*110g*) buckwheat flour
(ii) 8 oz. (*225g*) rye flour
(iii) 8 oz. (*225g*) barley flour

FRUCTOSE CREAM FILLING

Grind some fructose to a fine powder using a liquidiser, coffee grinder or food processor. Put 2 tblspns. milk-free margarine in a bowl and add a little ground fructose. Beat well and add more ground fructose, beating well after each addition, until required consistency is achieved.
(Store surplus ground fructose in a screw-top jar.)

VANILLA CREAM FILLING

Put 2 tblspns. milk-free margarine into a bowl. Add either icing sugar or ground fructose (see previous recipe). Add a little of the chosen sweetener at a time, beating well after each addition until the required consistency is achieved. Add a very little natural vanilla flavour and beat well. Check for flavour and use as required.

CHOCOLATE or CAROB FILLING

1 tblspn. milk-free margarine *or* oil of choice	1 tblspn. raw cocoa powder *or* carob powder
3 tblspns. icing sugar, glucose *or* finely ground fructose	1 tblspn. goats' *or* soya milk
	1–4 tblspns. powdered goats' *or* soya milk

Sieve cocoa or carob powder into a bowl. Add oil or margarine and beat. Add 1 tblspn. of sweetener and milk. Beat again and then add rest of sweetener and sufficient powdered milk to obtain required consistency. The amount of powdered milk required will vary depending upon whether margarine or oil has been used.

CHOCOLATE/CAROB AND HAZELNUT FILLING

1–2 tblspns. Hazelnut
Butter*

1–2 tspns. raw cocoa powder
or carob powder (sieved)

Put both ingredients into a mixing bowl and work together with a fork.

CAROB FROSTING (milk-free)

2 tblspns. water
3 oz. *(85g)* Foodwatch Carob
Buttons *or* Plamil Carob
Bar

1 oz. *(30g)* milk-free
margarine

Place the water and the carob buttons in a saucepan over a gentle heat, and stir until carob buttons have melted. Remove from heat and beat in the margarine. Allow to cool slightly and then spread over the top of the cake.

CHOCOLATE FROSTING (milk-free)

Use recipe and method for 'Carob Frosting' substituting Plamil Chocolate Bar *or* Bournville Plain Chocolate for Carob Buttons.

CAROB ICING

Gives a harder coating than the frosting and so is more suitable for biscuits, florentines and pastries.

3 oz. (*85g*) Foodwatch Carob Buttons

1 oz. (*30g*) milk-free margarine

Melt carob and margarine together over a gentle heat and beat until smooth. Use immediately, drawing the biscuit over the surface of the icing. Leave on a wire rack until set and then store in a tin.

SOYA MARZIPAN (egg-free)

5 oz. (*140g*) soft brown sugar, light
2 oz. (*55g*) soya flour
1 oz. (*30g*) milk-free margarine

½ tspn. natural almond essence
½ tblspn. water

Put all dry ingredients into a large mixing bowl and rub in the margarine until well incorporated. Add the almond essence and the water and mix until pliable, adding a little more water if necessary.

Pastries and Cold Desserts

SAGO SHORTCRUST PASTRY

9 oz. (255g) sago flour
4 oz. (110g) milk-free
  margarine

Pinch of salt
Approx. 2 tblspns. water

Sieve flour and salt into mixing bowl. Rub in the margarine until the mixture resembles fine breadcrumbs. Add sufficient water to mix until it clings together. If too sticky add a little more flour. Roll out pastry on sago flour and use as required. Bake at 200°C, 400°F, Gas Mark 6 until crisp or according to recipe used.

RICE PASTRY

2 oz. (*55g*) milk-free
   margarine
4 oz. (*110g*) brown rice flour

3 oz. (*85g*) eating apple,
   grated
Pinch of salt

Put all ingredients into a bowl and blend together with a fork. Knead until it forms a large ball of dough. Roll out on brown rice flour. Bake at 200°C, 400°F, Gas Mark 6 until crisp or according to recipe used.

PASTRY MADE WITH OIL

8 oz. (*225g*) rye, buckwheat,
   brown rice *or* chick pea
   flour
½ tspn. wheat-free baking
   powder

Pinch of salt
5 tblspns. oil
3 tblspns. cold water

Whisk oil and water together. Put all ingredients into a large mixing bowl and work together to form a soft dough.

As the dough is more difficult to handle than if it is made with a fat, put the ball of dough in the centre of the plate or flan dish and work it with the hands to cover the entire surface. Bake in the usual way.

BUCKWHEAT AND POTATO PASTRY

2 oz. (*55g*) milk-free
   margarine
2 oz. (*55g*) buckwheat flour
2 oz. (*55g*) potato flour

1 eating apple, grated
Pinch of salt

Put all ingredients into a bowl and blend with a fork. Knead until it forms a large ball of dough. Roll out or press into tin with the fingers. Bake at 180°C, 350°F, Gas Mark 4 for 15–20 minutes for individual tarts or 25–35 minutes for flans and plate pies. The temperature is a little lower than usual as this pastry tends to burn easily.

CHICK PEA AND POTATO PASTRY

Follow recipe and method for 'Buckwheat and Potato Pastry' substituting chick pea flour for buckwheat flour.

RICE AND POTATO PASTRY

3 oz. (85g) brown rice flour
1½ oz. (45g) soya flour
3 oz. (85g) potato flour

2 oz. (55g) milk-free margarine
2 tblspns. ground almonds *or* cashews
Water to mix

Put all ingredients into a bowl and blend with a fork, adding sufficient water to mix. Knead well. Roll out on brown rice flour, or for a plate tart, put the whole ball of pastry in the centre of the plate and press it flat, gradually working towards the edge of the plate. Bake at 200°C, 400°F, Gas Mark 6 until crisp or according to recipe used.

RYE SHORTCRUST PASTRY

8 oz. (*225g*) rye flour   2–3 tblspns. cold water
4 oz. (*110g*) milk-free   Pinch of salt
   margarine

Put the flour into a bowl and stir in salt. Rub in margarine until the mixture resembles fine breadcrumbs. Add sufficient water to mix. Bake at 200°C, 400°F, Gas Mark 6.

GUIDE FOR COOKING PASTRY

At 200°C, 400°F, Gas Mark 6 allow:-

For flans and plate pies ...... 25–35 minutes
For individual tarts .... 15–20 minutes

At lower temperatures allow a little longer.

DATE FLAN

Line a 7" or 8" flan tin with pastry of choice.

Filling: 2 tblspns. water
4 oz. (*110g*) dates

Chop the dates finely and put into a saucepan with the water. Simmer gently, stirring with a wooden spoon, until all liquid is absorbed and the mixture forms a smooth paste. Put into uncooked pastry case, smooth over the top with the back of a spoon. Decorate the top with leftover pastry cut into attractive shapes with mini-cutters, if desired. Bake at 190°C, 375°F, Gas Mark 5 for 35 minutes.
Serve with Coconut Cream*.

APRICOT FLAN

Line a 7" or 8" flan tin with pastry of choice.

4 oz. (*110g*) natural dried apricots

2 tblspns. water

Sweetener to taste

Proceed as for 'Date Flan' (previous recipe). If Hunza apricots are being used: Put apricots into a saucepan with just enough water to cover. Simmer gently until soft and then remove the stones. Drain off excess liquid and mash to a smooth paste.

BAKEWELL TART

Line a 7" or 8" flan tin with pastry of choice.

Filling:
2 oz. (*55g*) milk-free margarine
2 oz. (*55g*) demerara sugar, ground

1 egg
2 oz. (*55g*) ground almonds
Raspberry jam

Spread some raspberry jam in the base of the uncooked pastry case. Cream together margarine and sugar until light and fluffy. Beat egg and fold into mixture together with the ground almonds. Put into pastry case and smooth over the top. Bake at 200°C, 400°F, Gas Mark 6 for 25–30 minutes.

PEACHEESY FLAN

Line a 7″ or 8″ fluted flan ring on a baking tray with pastry of choice.

Filling:
2 large peaches
1 level tblspns cornflour *or*
    tapioca flour
1 level tspn. mixed spice
½ tspn. natural vanilla
    powder

Topping:
1 egg
2½ oz. (*70g*) caster sugar
2 tspns. lemon juice
2 tblspns. peach syrup
1 tblspn. goats' milk
1½ oz. (*45g*) soft goats'
    cheese *or* curd cheese*

Peel and slice peaches and poach lightly in a little sweetened water. Drain, reserving syrup. Put cornflour or tapioca flour, mixed spice and vanilla into a bowl and mix together. Add drained peaches and stir. Place peach mixture in flan case. Place egg, sugar, lemon juice and peach syrup in a small pan. Cook over a low heat, stirring until mixture thickens, but do not boil. Remove from the heat; beat in milk and soft cheese. Pour over peach mixture. Bake in centre of oven at 200°C, 400°F, Gas Mark 6 for 10 minutes and then reduce temperature to 180°C, 350°F, Gas Mark 4 and cook for a further 30–35 minutes, until topping is golden brown.
Serve hot or cold.

YOGHURT AND APRICOT FLAN

Line an 8″ or 9″ fluted flan ring with pastry of choice and place on a baking tray.

Filling:
8 oz. (*225g*) natural dried
    apricots, soaked
3 level tspns. gelatine
    (preservative-free) *or* 1½
    level tspns. agar agar

2 tblspns. hot water
1 egg white
10 fl.oz. (*250 ml*) natural
    goats' *or* sheep's yoghurt

Decoration:
Foodwatch Whipped
Topping

3 fresh apricots *or* drained
canned apricots
A few flaked almonds

Bake the pastry case 'blind' for 15 minutes at 190°C, 375°F, Gas Mark 5. Remove the baking beans and bake, uncovered, for a further 5 minutes. Cook the soaked apricots for 20 minutes in the soaking water. Purée the fruit. Dissolve the gelatine or agar agar in the hot water. Stir in the apricot purée. Fold in the yoghurt. Whisk egg whites and fold into apricot mixture. Pour into the baked and cooled flan case and leave to set. Halve and stone the fresh apricots or use 6 tinned apricot halves. Place the apricot halves at equal distances around edge of flan. Put a whirl of whipped topping between each apricot half and stand a couple of flakes of almond in each squirl.

BAKED CHEESECAKE

1 quantity of pastry, using 6 oz. (*170g*) flour of choice.

Filling:
1 lb. (*450g*) goats' *or* sheep's
    curd cheese*
1 egg white, beaten

4 oz. (*110g*) sugar
1 oz. (*30g*) natural sultanas

Line the bottom of a 7″ square tin with two thirds of the pastry. Roll out rest of pastry and cut into 9″ strips about ¼″ wide. Place all ingredients for filling in a bowl and mix well. Turn into pastry-lined tin, and arrange pastry strips in a lattice pattern. Brush pastry with goats' or sheep's milk. Bake for 45–50 minutes at 190°C, 375°F, Gas Mark 5. Cool for 30 minutes in tin, then when really set take out and put on a wire rack.
Cut into 2″ squares and serve.

CHEESECAKE

4 oz. (*110g*) Sweet Biscuits*
  or Shortbread*
2 oz. (*55g*) milk-free
  margarine
2 level tspns. gelatine
  (preservative-free) *or*
  1 level tspn. agar agar
1½ tblspns. very hot water

1 large egg yolk
2 oz. (*55g*) caster sugar *or*
  1 oz. (*30g*) fructose
6 oz. (*170g*) soft goats'
  cheese *or* curd cheese*
3 fl.oz. (*75 ml*) goats' *or*
  sheep's milk
1 large lemon

Put the biscuits into a large plastic bag and crush with a rolling pin. Melt margarine in a saucepan and stir in the biscuit crumbs. Lightly grease a loose-bottomed cake tin. Spoon biscuit mixture into cake tin and press down well with a potato masher. Chill in refrigerator for two hours. Dissolve the gelatine or agar agar in the hot water and leave to cool but not set. Put egg yolk, sugar or fructose, cheese and milk into liquidiser and mix for 1 minute. Squeeze the juice from ½ the lemon and add 3 tblspns. to the liquidiser along with the cooled gelatine or agar agar and mix again. Pour this mixture onto the set biscuit base in the cake tin and return to the refrigerator for a further two hours. Just before serving, thinly slice the remaining ½ lemon and cut each slice in half. Arrange around outside edge of cheesecake.

Slices of Kiwi Fruit make a very attractive alternative decoration.

To remove from tin: Place tin on top of a container such as a tin of treacle and very gently draw down the sides of the cake tin. Transfer to serving plate using a palette knife to ease the cheesecake from the cake tin base.

FRUIT TOPPED CHEESECAKE

Use previous recipe leaving out lemon, if desired. These are usually topped with cherries or pineapple but any fruit is suitable (tinned, bottled, frozen or fresh). Before removing the cheesecake from the tin decorate the top with fruit of choice. Blend 1 rounded tspn. cornflour, sago or tapioca flour with 5 tblspns. juice in a saucepan. Bring to the boil, then stir over a low heat for 1 minute. Spoon over fruit and leave to set. Remove from tin as described at end of previous recipe.

CASSATA CHEESE PEARS

Serves 3

3 large Comice or William
    pears
Juice of 1 lemon
4 oz. (110g) goats' cheese or
    curd cheese*
1 oz. (30g) diced papaya or
    mango pieces, chopped

1 oz. (30g) natural currants
1 oz. (30g) natural sultanas
Parsley

Cut a small slice off the top of each pear. Remove 5 thin strips of peel, forming ridges from top to bottom and brush with lemon juice. Carefully remove cores, and brush inside with lemon juice. Combine cheese and fruits and pile into hollow centres and in a small mound on top of each pear. Stand pears on individual dishes and top each with a tiny sprig of parsley. Serve as a starter or a dessert.

HAWAIIAN PINEAPPLE

Serves 4

1 small ripe pineapple
8 strawberries *or*
  raspberries to decorate

½ lb. *(225g)* goats' *or* sheep's
  curd cheese* *or* soft goats'
  cheese

Wash pineapple and other fruit. Dry on kitchen paper.

Cut pineapple into quarters lengthways, scoop out flesh and chop. Place cheese in a bowl and stir in pineapple. Pile into pineapple 'shells' and decorate each with strawberries or raspberries. Place on a serving dish and keep cool until ready to serve.

PASHKA

This is an adaptation of a traditional Russian recipe. The original contained cow's milk cheese, candied peel and glacé cherries.

1 pt. *(500 ml)* goats' *or*
  sheep's curd cheese*
2 oz. *(55g)* milk-free
  margarine
1 oz. *(30g)* diced papaya,
  chopped mango *or*
  jackfruit in cane sugar

1 oz. *(30g)* crystallised *or*
  stem ginger, diced
1 oz. *(30g)* flaked almonds *or*
  hazelnuts
2 egg yolks
1 or 2 tblspns. goats' *or*
  sheep's yoghurt
A little sugar *or* fructose

Sieve the curd cheese into a bowl. Work in the margarine. Add fruit and nuts and mix well. Beat egg yolks with a little sugar or fructose and stir in well together with the yoghurt. Line a large sieve with two layers of muslin and stand this over a bowl. Fill with the mixture. Flatten the top and fold the muslin over the top to enclose the mixture. Cover with a weighted plate. Place in the refrigerator and leave overnight, by which time all the excess liquid will have drained into the bowl. Turn out onto a serving dish and decorate with strips and small pieces of dried fruits of different colours.

ORANGE JELLY

4 level tspns. gelatine
(preservative-free) *or*
2 level tspns. agar agar
¼ pt. (*125 ml*) hot water
3 tblspns. lemon juice,
freshly squeezed

½ pt. (*250 ml*) orange juice,
freshly squeezed
3 oz. (*85g*) sugar *or* 1½ oz.
(*40g*) fructose

Add gelatine or agar agar to hot water and stir until dissolved. Allow to cool. Mix with all other ingredients and place in a rinsed mould. Leave in refrigerator to set.

FRUIT JELLY

4 level tspns. gelatine
(preservative-free) *or*
2 level tspns. agar agar
¼ pt. (*125 ml*) hot water

¾ pt. (*375 ml*) pure fruit juice
3–4 oz. (*85–110g*) sugar,
according to taste

Add gelatine or agar agar to hot water and stir until dissolved. Allow to cool. Mix with all other ingredients and place in mould. Leave to set in refrigerator.

If using Foodwatch Fruit Juice Concentrate: put 4 or 5 tspns. in ¾ pt. (*375 ml*) water and use instead of ¾ pt. fruit juice.

MANDARIN ORANGE JELLY

1 tin mandarin orange
segments in natural juice

4 level tspns. gelatine
(preservative-free) *or*
2 level tspns. agar agar

Dissolve the gelatine or agar agar in a little hot water. Leave to cool. Meanwhile, empty the contents of the tin into a liquidiser goblet and blend until smooth. Pour both mixtures into a 1 pt. measuring jug and top up to 1 pt. with cold water. Pour into a 1 pt. bowl or jelly mould and leave in the refrigerator to set.

Other tasty fruits in natural juice are also good for making jelly in this way.

MILK JELLY

4 level tspns. gelatine
(preservative-free) or
2 level tspns. agar agar
3 tblspns. very hot water

¾ pt. (375 ml) goats',
sheep's, soya or nut milk*
2 tblspns. sugar or 1 tblspn.
fructose

Dissolve gelatine or agar agar in hot water and allow to cool. Add sweetener and gradually stir in milk. Pour into mould or serving dish and leave in refrigerator to set.
Serve with fruit.

FRUIT MOUSSE

4 level tspns. gelatine
(preservative-free) or
2 level tspns. agar agar
3 tblspns. very hot water
2 eggs

Small pinch of salt
1 pt. (500 ml) fruit purée
Sweetener to taste

Dissolve gelatine or agar agar in hot water. Beat egg yolks thoroughly. Add sweetened fruit purée. Stir over hot water until quite hot. Leave to cool. Add dissolved gelatine or agar agar. Add salt to egg whites and beat until stiff. Fold into mixture and pour into serving bowl. Leave in refrigerator to set.

CAROB OR CHOCOLATE DESSERT

¾–1 pt. (*375–500 ml*) goats',
   sheep's *or* soya milk
4 level tspns. gelatine
   (preservative-free) *or*
   2 level tspns. agar agar
2 tblspns. maple syrup

1 tblspn. carob *or* raw cocoa
   powder
A few drops of natural
   vanilla essence *or* a pinch
   of natural vanilla powder

Dissolve the gelatine or agar agar in a little hot water. When dissolved mix with sufficient milk to make up to 1 pt. (*500 ml*). Pour into liquidiser along with the rest of the ingredients and blend until smooth. Pour into a dish or mould and chill until set.

SPANISH CREAM

4 level tspns. gelatine
   (preservative-free) *or*
   2 level tspns. agar agar
3 tblspns. very hot water
2 eggs
3 tblspns. sugar *or* 1½
   tblspns. fructose

Pinch of salt
¾ pt. (*375 ml*) goats' *or*
   sheep's milk
Piece of vanilla pod *or* pinch
   of natural vanilla flavour

(If using vanilla pod, leave in milk while it is hot and then remove).

Beat egg yolk lightly. Add sugar or fructose and salt to milk, heat until nearly boiling, pour over beaten eggs and return to heat. Cook until the mixture thickens and breaks into curds and whey. (If separation is not required, do not boil the custard. Heat gently until the mixture thickens). Dissolve the gelatine or agar agar in the hot water, and add carefully to mixture. Beat egg whites until stiff and fold into the mixture. Place in a mould and leave to set in refrigerator.

APRICOT CREAM

8 oz. (*225g*) natural dried
   apricots
2½ fl.oz. (*60 ml*) water
2–3 oz. (*55–85g*) sugar,
   according to taste

3 egg yolks
3 level tblspns. cornflour *or*
   arrowroot
1 pt. (*500 ml*) goats' *or*
   sheep's milk

Simmer apricots with water and sugar until soft and smooth, and then rub through a sieve. Mix flour with a little milk. Bring rest of milk to the boil. Pour over flour and return to pan to thicken, stirring well. Add sweetened purée whisked with the egg yolks. Continue cooking gently until thick, but do not allow to boil. Pour into serving dish and leave to set.

FRUIT FOOL

8 oz. (*225g*) soft fruit
   (gooseberries,
   blackcurrants,
   raspberries,
   strawberries,
   blackberries etc.)
2½ fl.oz. (*60 ml*) water
2–3 oz. (*55–85g*) sugar,
   according to taste

3 egg yolks
2 level tblspns. cornflour *or*
   arrowroot
1 pt. (*500 ml*) goats' *or*
   sheep's milk
Fresh fruit for decoration

Simmer the fruit with the water and sugar until very soft and smooth. Sieve or purée the cooked fruit. Blend cornflour or arrowroot with a little milk. Bring rest of the milk to the boil. Pour over mixed flour, stirring well, and return to pan to thicken. Add sweetened purée whisked with egg yolks. Continue cooking gently until thick, but do not allow to boil as mixture will curdle. Pour into rinsed mould or individual dishes. Before serving decorate with reserved fruit.

ICE-CREAM-TYPE DESSERT

1 pt. (*500 ml*) goats' *or*
   sheep's milk
2 eggs
3 oz. (*85g*) sugar or 2 oz.
   (*55g*) fructose
1 tspn. gelatine
   (preservative-free) *or*
   ½ tspn. agar agar

2 tblspns. very hot water
Piece of vanilla pod *or* pinch
   of natural vanilla flavour

(If using vanilla pod, leave in milk while it is hot and then remove.)

Turn control knob on refrigerator to coldest position. Measure ½ pt (*250 ml*) of the milk. Beat eggs with a little of the first ½ pt. and boil remainder of this ½ pt. Pour over eggs and stir well. Strain into saucepan and cook gently (do not allow to boil), stirring continuously until custard coats back of spoon. Leave to cool. Dissolve gelatine or agar agar in hot water and add to custard, with the sugar or fructose. Stir in the second ½ pt. of milk. Pour into ice trays and place in icemaking compartment of the fridge. When the mixture is firm round the edges, turn into a chilled bowl and beat thoroughly. Return to ice trays and freeze till firm.

Variations:
CHOCOLATE – dissolve 3½ oz. (*100g*) Bournville Plain chocolate in a little of the milk.
CAROB – dissolve 3½ oz. (*100g*) Plamil Carob Bar in a little of the milk.
COFFEE – dissolve 1 tblspn. Nescafé granules in a little milk.
COFFEE SUBSTITUTE – dissolve 1 tblspn. 'Pionier' coffee substitute in a little of the milk.
FRUIT – add ½ pt. (*250 ml*) fruit purée instead of second ½ pt. (*250 ml*) milk. Add extra sugar or fructose to taste.
TUTTI FRUTTI – mix 4 oz. (*110g*) dried fruit and nuts into the mixture before the final freezing.
ROSE – add a little distilled Rose Water to taste.

RASPBERRY SORBET

8 oz. (*225g*) raspberries
10 fl.oz. (*250 ml*) goats' *or*
   sheep's yoghurt
1 tblspn. lemon juice

2 level tspns. gelatine
   (preservative-free) *or*
   1 level tspn. agar agar
2 egg whites
Sweetener to taste

Mash and sieve the raspberries. Mix purée with yoghurt and lemon juice. Dissolve the gelatine or agar agar in a little hot water, stir into purée and sweeten to taste. Whisk the egg whites until stiff and carefully fold into fruit mixture. Pour into containers and freeze.

To serve: Thaw for a short while in the fridge to bring out the flavour.

CHOCOLATE OR CAROB BLANCMANGE

3 level tblspns. cornflour *or*
   arrowroot
1 level tblspn. raw cocoa
   powder *or* carob powder

1–2 level tblspns. sugar *or*
   ½–1 level tblspn. fructose
1 pt. (*570 ml*) goats' *or*
   sheep's milk

Use the smaller amount of sweetener if using carob powder and the larger amount of sweetener if using raw cocoa powder.

Blend dry ingredients with a little of the cold milk. Bring the rest of the milk to the boil and pour over the mixture, stirring well. Return to heat to thicken and then simmer for 2–3 minutes. Pour into serving dish and leave to cool. Put into the refrigerator to set.

ARROWROOT BLANCMANGE

4 heaped tblspns. arrowroot
1½ tblspns. sugar *or*
¾ tblspn. fructose

1½ pt. (*750 ml*) goats',
sheep's *or* soya milk
A few drops of natural
vanilla essence

Put arrowroot and sweetener into a bowl or jug; add a little of the measured milk and mix well. Meanwhile, put rest of the milk on to boil. Pour boiling milk over arrowroot, stirring all the time. Return to pan and heat, stirring all the time, until thick. Simmer gently for 2–3 minutes. Remove from heat and stir in flavouring. Pour into a serving bowl and chill until set.

Alternative: any other natural flavouring may be used.

Serve with stewed fruit or fresh fruit salad.

GRAPE DESSERT

1 pt. (*500 ml*) grape juice
6 level tblspns. arrowroot

Sweetener of choice
Fresh grapes

Skin, deseed and chop some fresh grapes. Put arrowroot into a bowl and add a little of the measured grape juice. Put the rest of the grape juice in a saucepan and bring to the boil. Pour over the mixed arrowroot and stir well. Return to pan and heat, stirring all the time, until thick. Simmer for 2–3 minutes. Remove from the heat and stir in the chopped grapes and sweeten to taste. Pour into individual sundae dishes and leave to set. When ready to serve decorate with a few halved and deseeded grapes.

Alternative: any other juice and fruit.

CHOCOLATE OR CAROB MILLET CRÈME

2¼ oz. (*65g*) millet flakes
2 oz. (*55g*) natural raisins
2 level tblspns. sugar *or*
    honey

2 level tblspns. pure cocoa
    powder *or* carob powder
1 pt. (*500 ml*) goats', sheep's
    or soya milk

Pour milk into non-stick pan. Add millet flakes, sweetener and raisins. Mix cocoa or carob into a paste with a little of the milk and then add it to saucepan. Bring the mixture to the boil, stirring, and cook gently for 6–10 minutes until creamy. Remove from heat and cool. Pour into individual glasses or dishes and leave to set.

PEAR AND MILLET DESSERT

Serves 4

8 oz. (*225g*) whole millet
2 oz. (*55g*) demerara *or*
    maple sugar
1 pt. (*500 ml*) goats' *or*
    sheep's milk

2 large pears
Almond *or* hazelnut flakes
Chocolate *or* carob sauce*

Combine the millet, sugar and milk in a pan. Bring to the boil and simmer gently for 30 minutes. Cool the mixture and then divide between 4 sundae dishes. Leave until completely cold. Just before serving, peel, core and halve the pears putting half into each dish. Cover with chocolate or carob sauce and sprinkle with flaked nuts.

RHUBARB AND GINGER WHIP

Serves 4

1¼ lb. (*560g*) rhubarb
2 tblspns. clear honey
1 piece stem *or* crystallised
  ginger

8 fl.oz. (*200 ml*) sheep's
  yoghurt
1 oz. (*30g*) flaked almonds

Trim rhubarb, removing any coarse stringy pieces. Cut into ½" lengths and cook gently with a little water until soft. Sweeten with honey.* Finely chop the stem ginger and stir into the rhubarb. Gently fold in the yoghurt and divide between four serving dishes. Sprinkle flaked almonds over the top.

Alternative: Silken Tofu may be used instead of sheep's yoghurt. In which case, follow the above instructions down to the *. Put the silken tofu into a blender or liquidiser and add the rhubarb mixture and blend. Stir in the finely chopped ginger and divide between four serving dishes. Sprinkle flaked almonds over the top.

PRUNE AND TOFU DESSERT

Serves 4

4 oz. (*110g*) unsorbated
  prunes
8 oz. (*225g*) tofu

2 tblspns. maple syrup *or*
  date syrup *or* clear honey

Soak the prunes overnight. Drain and place in a saucepan with sufficient fresh water to cover. Simmer for 10–15 minutes until really tender. Drain again (reserving the liquor) and place in a liquidiser together with the tofu and sweetener of choice. Blend. Add just enough of the cooking liquor to make a thick but soft purée and reblend. Pour into 4 sundae glasses and chill until ready to serve.

APRICOT AND TOFU DESSERT

Follow recipe and method for 'Prune and Tofu Dessert' substituting natural dried apricots for prunes.

CREAMY FRUIT CONDÉ

Serves 4

Make a 1 lb. (*450g*) rice, tapioca *or* sago pudding using goats', sheep's, soya *or* nut milk* and leave until cold.

3 rounded tspns. gelatine *or*	1 lb. (*450g*) fresh tasty fruit
1½ tspns. agar agar	such as raspberries

Dissolve gelatine or agar agar in a little hot water and when dissolved make up to ¾ pt. (*375 ml*) with cold water. Add a little lemon juice to flavour, if wished. Put half the fruit in a bowl and reserve the rest for decoration. Either chop or slightly mash the fruit according to type. Mix the cold pudding, fruit and ½ pt. (*250 ml*) of the cooled jelly and pour into 4 individual sundae dishes. Pop into the refrigerator until just set. Arrange remainder of the fruit on top and spoon the other ¼ pt. (*125 ml*) of jelly over the fruit to glaze. Put in refrigerator until set.

A delicious alternative is to use tinned green figs (15 oz./425g) *or* fresh figs, poached and 3 oz. (*85g*) natural sultanas.

GOLDEN LAYER DESSERT

6 oz. (*170g*) natural dried
  apricots
½ pt. (*250 ml*) water
2 oz. (*55g*) demerara sugar
2 egg whites
1 oz. (*30g*) Foodwatch
  Custard Powder
1¼ pts. (*625 ml*) goats',
  sheep's *or* soya milk
1 oz. (*30g*) demerara sugar
¼ tspn. natural vanilla
  flavour

To decorate:
Foodwatch Whipped
  Topping
Foodwatch Chocolate Sugar
  Strands

Stew the apricots with the water and 2 oz. demerara sugar until very soft. Put into a liquidiser and blend until smooth, or rub through a sieve. When cold, fold in stiffly beaten egg whites. Mix the custard powder to a smooth paste with a little of the milk, add the rest and bring to the boil, stirring. Boil for 2–3 minutes, remove from the heat and stir in the 1 oz. (*30g*) demerara sugar and natural vanilla flavour.

Pour into serving dish and leave until cold and set. Cover with the fruit mixture and decorate with whipped topping and chocolate sugar strands.

RUM ALMONDEEN

Bake a brown rice flour sponge cake in a 6" lined loose-bottomed cake tin and use as a base for this rum flavoured dessert.

1½ oz. (45g) blanched almonds	2 oz. (55g) soft goats' cheese *or* curd cheese*
2 oz. (55g) milk-free margarine	1 dessertspoon rum
1½ oz. (45g) icing sugar	5 fl.oz. (125 ml) carton goats' yoghurt
1 egg	2 tblspns. goats' milk

Using the same cake tin as above, line base with foil and line sides with a 1½" strip of foil. Slice 2 x ½" circles off bottom of cake (remainder could be used for a trifle).

Prepare a moderate grill. Place almonds on grill pan and toast until golden brown. Reserve 6 almonds for decoration and chop remainder finely. Cream margarine and icing sugar together in a bowl until light and fluffy. Separate egg; place white in a separate bowl. Beat yolk into margarine mixture. Sieve soft cheese and beat into margarine mixture with the rum. Stir yoghurt in the carton. Fold in half the yoghurt, reserving rest for decoration. Whisk egg whites until stiff but not dry. Fold egg whites and almonds into mixture. Place one sponge circle in base of lined tin. Spoon 1 tblspn. (15 ml) goats' milk all over the cake. Spread half of the almond and rum mixture over the cake. Next add second sponge circle and soak with goats' milk as before. Spread remaining almond and rum mixture on top. Leave in fridge to set. Invert tin on a serving plate and carefully remove tin and foil. Spread the rest of the yoghurt over the top of the Rum Almondeen and decorate with reserved almonds. Chill until ready to serve.

Hot Puddings
and
Sweet Sauces

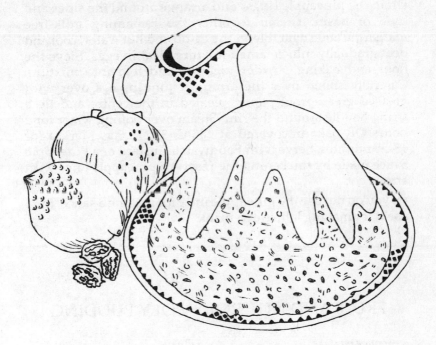

PINEAPPLE UPSIDE-DOWN PUDDING

A gluten-free version of an old favourite.

7 oz. (*200 g*) milk-free
margarine

2 tblspns. hot water
3 eggs

15½ oz. (435g) can
  pineapple rings in
  natural juice
6½ oz. (185g) demerara
  sugar
2 tblspns. carob powder

6 oz. (170g) brown rice flour
2 level tspns. wheat-free
  baking powder

Grease a 2 pt. pudding basin with 1 oz. (30g) milk-free margarine and then sprinkle with ½ oz. (15g) demerara sugar. Drain the pineapple rings* and arrange around the sides and base of basin. Cream together the remaining milk-free margarine and sugar. Blend the carob and hot water, cool and beat gradually into creamed mixture. Beat in eggs. Sieve the flour and baking powder together and fold into mixture. Carefully spoon over the arranged pineapple. Cover with greased greaseproof paper, pleated in the centre and tie a string handle around the rim. Steam over boiling water for 2 hours OR bake uncovered at 180°C, 350°F, Gas Mark 4 for 45–55 minutes. Serve with Foodwatch Custard or a Pineapple Sauce made by thickening the reserved pineapple juice with arrowroot.

* If you do not use the pineapple juice for making a sauce, then use it for making lollies or a drink.

FRUIT AND NUT ROLY-POLY PUDDING

Sponge mixture:
2 eggs
2 oz. (55g) demerara sugar,
  ground
3 oz. (85g) ground nuts,
  toasted
1 oz. (30g) brown rice flour,
  buckwheat flour, banana
  flour *or* chick pea flour

Filling:
3 oz. (85g) roughly chopped
  nuts, toasted
1 lb. (450g) fruit purée of
  choice

Make the fruit purée first by simmering fruit of choice until soft. Leave to cool and then rub through a fine-meshed sieve. Sweeten to taste. Brush a Swiss-Roll tin with oil of choice and line with oiled greaseproof paper. Whisk the eggs and sugar in a bowl over a pan of simmering water until they are pale and thick and the mixture leaves a trail. Remove from the heat and cool a little. Fold in the flour and nuts. Pour the mixture into the prepared tin. Bake at 220°C, 425°F, Gas Mark 7 for 12 minutes only. Dredge some sugar onto a sheet of greaseproof paper and turn the sponge out onto this. Quickly spread some of the fruit purée onto the sponge and sprinkle with the chopped nuts. Roll up the sponge using the paper to help you. Serve immediately with the rest of the fruit purée served in a sauce boat.

Suggested fruit and nut combinations:
Apricot, plums *or* cherries with almonds
Raspberries *or* loganberries with hazelnuts
Gooseberries *or* blackcurrants with cashews

FAT-FREE MINI SPONGES

Makes 10–12

2½ oz. (*70g*) brown rice flour, buckwheat flour, banana flour *or* chick pea flour

3 eggs
3 oz. (*85g*) demerara sugar, ground

Brush 10–12 bun tins or fancy moulds with oil of choice. Dredge the inside of each tin with sugar, shaking away any excess. Mix the sugar and eggs in a bowl which will sit comfortably inside the top of a pan of simmering water. Using a rotary whisk, whisk the mixture until it is pale, thick and leaves a trail. Remove the basin from the heat and continue whisking gently until the mixture cools a little. Gently fold in the flour. Spoon the mixture into the prepared tins, filling them approximately two-thirds full. Sprinkle a good pinch of sugar on top. Bake at 180°C, 350°F, Gas Mark 4 for 12–15 minutes, when the puddings should be firm to the touch. Serve hot or cold with a fruit sauce or stewed fruit.

BAKED RICE FLOUR SPONGE PUDDING

Use Rice Flour Sponge Cake* recipe, but increase the amount of brown rice flour to 6 oz. (*170g*).

Grease or oil a pudding basin and put either jam or half quantity of Fruit Filling* recipe into base of the dish and top with the sponge mixture. Bake at 180°C, 350°F, Gas Mark 4 for 45–55 minutes.

Variations: To the sponge mixture add (i) a chopped apple (ii) natural raisins or sultanas (iii) chopped dates (iv) chopped figs or (v) grated lemon rind.

STEAMED RICE FLOUR SPONGE PUDDING

Make as for previous recipe. Fill greased or oiled pudding basin. Cover with foil or greaseproof paper and tie tightly with string and make a string handle. Steam in a large pan of boiling water for 1½–2 hours. Ensure that the pan does not boil dry.

BAKED CHOCOLATE OR CAROB SPONGE PUDDING

Use the recipe for Mud Huts*, but increase the amount of flour to 6 oz. (*170g*).

Grease or oil a pudding basin and put in mixture. Bake at 180°C, 350°F, Gas Mark 4 for 45–55 minutes.

Serve with Chocolate or Carob Sauce*.

STEAMED CHOCOLATE OR CAROB SPONGE PUDDING

Make as for previous recipe. Cover basin with foil or greaseproof paper and tie tightly with string. Make a string handle. Steam in a large pan of boiling water for 1½–2 hours. Ensure that the pan does not boil dry.

FRUIT FILLING (for puddings and crumbles)

½ lb. (*225g*) fruit of choice
A little water
Sweetener to taste

1 tblspn. flour (use same flour as for pudding or crumble mixture)

Put fruit and a little water in saucepan and cook until soft. Mash with a fork. Sweeten to taste. Add flour mixed with a little water and stir while cooking until mixture thickens.

SAGO FRUIT CRUMBLE

8 oz. (*225g*) sago flour
3½ oz. (*100g*) milk-free
    margarine

3 oz. (*85g*) sugar
½ quantity of Fruit Filling*

Brush the inside of a pie dish with melted margarine. Then place prepared fruit filling in the dish. Sieve the flour into a mixing bowl and rub in the margarine until the mixture resembles breadcrumbs. Stir in the sugar. Place the crumble mixture over the top of the fruit and smooth over with the back of a spoon. Bake at 180°C, 350°F, Gas Mark 4 for about 35 minutes or until the crumble is golden brown.

TAPIOCA FRUIT CRUMBLE

8 oz. (*225g*) tapioca flour
5 oz. (*140g*) milk-free
    margarine

3 oz. (*85g*) sugar
½ quantity of Fruit Filling*

Method as for Sago Fruit Crumble* substituting tapioca flour for sago flour to thicken fruit.

SWEET POTATO FRUIT CRUMBLE

4 oz. (*110g*) sweet potato
    flour
2 oz. (*55g*) milk-free
    margarine

3 oz. (*85g*) demerara sugar
½ quantity of Fruit Filling*

Method as for Sago Fruit Crumble* substituting sweet potato flour for sago flour to thicken fruit. Bake at 190°C, 375°F, Gas Mark 5 for 25–30 minutes.

DATE CRUMBLE

4 oz. *(110g)* brown rice flour *or* barley flour	3 oz. *(85g)* demerara sugar *or* 2 oz. *(55g)* fructose
2 oz. *(55g)* milk-free margarine	4 oz. *(110g)* dates
	2 tblspns. water

Chop dates finely and put into a saucepan with the water. Simmer gently, stirring with a wooden spoon, until all liquid is absorbed and the mixture forms a smooth paste. Put into the bottom of a greased shallow dish and smooth with the back of a spoon. Rub together flour and margarine until it resembles breadcrumbs, and then stir in sugar or fructose. Put this mixture over the dates. Bake at 190°C, 375°F, Gas Mark 5 for 25–30 minutes.

APRICOT AND PRUNE PUDDING

4 oz. *(110g)* natural dried apricots	1 lemon
4 oz. *(110g)* unsorbated prunes	2 oz. *(55g)* walnuts
¼ pt. *(125 ml)* apple *or* grape juice	2 oz. *(55g)* soft goats' cheese *or* curd cheese*
	1 oz. *(30g)* sugar *or* ½ oz. *(15g)* fructose

Put the apricots and prunes into a basin and pour the apple or grape juice over them. Add water until liquid just covers the fruit. Leave overnight.

Finely grate the lemon rind and squeeze out the juice. Chop walnuts. In a small bowl, beat together the lemon rind, juice, cheese and sugar. Stir in the chopped walnuts. Drain the fruit and* remove the stones. Put half the fruit in the base of an ovenproof dish. Cover with the lemon cheese mixture and cover with the remainder of the fruit.

Top with a sponge or crumble mixture and bake at 180°C, 350°F, Gas Mark 4 for 45–55 minutes for a sponge OR follow the baking instructions given for the type of crumble used.

*Use the drained liquor to make a sauce using 1 dessertspoonful arrowroot to ½ pt. liquor.

BAKED BARLEY PUDDING

4 oz. (*110g*) barley flakes
2 oz. (*55g*) barley flour
2 oz. (*55g*) demerara sugar
2 tblspns. black treacle
½ tspn. mixed spice
2 eggs
1 oz. (*30g*) vegetable suet
   with rice flour

½ tspn. wheat-free baking
   powder
2 oz. (*55g*) natural sultanas
2 oz. (*55g*) ground almonds
½ tspn. ground ginger
¼ pt. (*125 ml*) goats',
   sheep's, soya *or* nut milk*

Mix all dry ingredients together. Stir in the vegetable suet. Beat eggs and add together with the milk and treacle. Mix well and cook at 190°C, 375°F, Gas Mark 5 for 1 hour; turn down heat to 180°C, 350°F, Gas Mark 4 and continue to cook for a further 45 minutes – 1 hour until firm to the touch.
Serve with Foodwatch Custard.

APRICOT AND RYE PUDDING

Serves 4

2 oz. (*55g*) natural dried
   apricots
2 oz. (*55g*) rye flakes
2 tblspns. clear honey

¾ pt. (*375 ml*) goats' *or*
   sheep's milk
1 egg, beaten

Place the apricots in a bowl, cover with water and leave overnight to soak. Liquidise the soaked apricots with ¼ pt. (*125 ml*) soaking liquor. Spoon into a shallow, greased or oiled ovenproof dish. Lightly toast the rye flakes. Mix together with 1 tblspn. (*15 ml*) honey, the milk and egg. Pour gently over the apricot purée. Stand the dish on a baking sheet and bake at 170°C, 325°F, Gas Mark 3 for about 45 minutes or until a skin has formed. Drizzle over the remainder of the honey and continue to bake for a further 15 minutes. Serve warm.

PRUNE AND BARLEY PUDDING

Follow recipe and method for 'Apricot and Rye Pudding' substituting prunes for apricots and barley flakes for rye flakes.

CREAMED RICE PUDDING

Serves 4

3 oz. (*85g*) brown rice flakes
1½ pts. (*750 ml*) goats' *or*
   sheep's milk

2 oz. (*55g*) sugar *or* 1¼ oz.
   (*40g*) fructose
Piece of vanilla pod *or* pinch
   of natural vanilla flavour

(If using vanilla pod, leave in milk for a few minutes while it is hot and then remove.)

Bring the rice flakes and milk slowly to the boil in a saucepan. Cook gently for 8–10 minutes. Remove from heat and stir in rest of ingredients. This recipe makes a thin pudding. If you prefer a thicker pudding then use a little less milk.

FRUITY CREAMED RICE PUDDING

Follow the previous recipe but use a little less milk to cook, then stir in chopped, canned or bottled fruit with some of the juice or chopped fresh fruit with their own juice.

RAISIN 'N' RICE PUDDING

Follow the recipe for Creamed Rice Pudding* and add 2 oz. (*55g*) natural raisins. Reduce the amount of sweetener by half.

BAKED RICE PUDDING

Serves 4

3 oz. (*85g*) brown rice flakes
2 oz. (*55g*) sugar *or* 1 oz. (*30g*)
  fructose
1½ pts. (*750 ml*) goats' *or*
  sheep's milk

1 oz. (*30g*) milk-free
  margarine
A little grated nutmeg
  (optional)

Put rice flakes, sugar or fructose and milk into a 2 pt. pie dish. Leave for an hour, if possible, then stir well. Float knobs of margarine all over the top and place in oven at 150°C, 300°F, Gas Mark 2 for about ½ hour, or until pudding is rising in large bubbles all over. Lower heat to 140°C, 275°F, Gas Mark 1 and continue cooking for another ½ hour.

Grated nutmeg may be sprinkled over the pudding before baking, if desired.

MILLET PUDDING

Serves 3

1 pt. (*250 ml*) hot goats',
  sheep's *or* soya milk
2 tblspns. millet flakes
1 egg, beaten
3 tblspns. honey *or* maple
  syrup

½ tblspn. soya flour
½ tspn. ground nutmeg
Pinch of salt
½ pt. (*250 ml*) cold milk (as
  above)

Blend hot milk and millet flakes. In a separate container blend the rest of the ingredients, except the nutmeg, then combine the two mixtures and turn into greased or oiled custard cups or pie dish. Dust top with nutmeg. Bake at 180°C, 350°F, Gas Mark 4 until set, about 30 minutes.

FRUIT AND NUT MILLET PUDDING

1 pt. (*500 ml*) goats', sheep's or soya milk
3½ oz. (*100g*) millet flakes
1 knob milk-free margarine
4 tblspns. ground almonds

2 eggs, separated
2 tblspns. sugar or honey
Grated rind of lemon (optional)
2 tblspns. natural raisins or sultanas

Heat milk, millet flakes, and knob of margarine in a saucepan until boiling. Let it cool. Add egg yolks, sugar or honey, lemon rind, raisins and nuts. Finally, gently fold in stiffly beaten egg whites. Put into a greased or oiled pie dish and bake at 200°C, 400°F, Gas Mark 6 for 20–25 minutes.

SPICY MILLET PUDDING

8 oz. (*225g*) whole millet
1 level tspn. ground cinnamon
1 pt. (*500 ml*) goats' or sheep's milk

2 oz. (*55g*) muscovado or demerara sugar
2 tblspns. natural sultanas (optional)

Combine milk and millet with the sugar and spice in a saucepan. Bring to the boil and simmer for 10 minutes. Transfer to a greased or oiled ovenproof dish, stir in dried fruit, if using, and bake at 180°C, 350°F, Gas Mark 4 for 20 minutes.

SPICY SORGHUM PUDDING

Follow the recipe for 'Spicy Millet Pudding' substituting sorghum for millet. You may find that you have to add a little more milk during the simmering stage, as sorghum absorbs more liquid than millet does. It also takes longer to cook, so simmer for 40 minutes. Transfer to a greased or oiled ovenproof dish, stir in dried fruit, if using, and bake at 180°C, 350°F, Gas Mark 4 for 20 minutes.

BAKED ARROWROOT PUDDING

1 pt. (*500 ml*) goats', sheep's
   or soya milk
1 tblspn. arrowroot

1 tblspn. sugar *or* ½ tblspn.
   fructose
3 eggs

Put the arrowroot and sweetener of choice into a bowl. Add a little of the measured milk and mix well. Meanwhile, put the rest of the milk on to boil. Pour boiling milk over arrowroot, stirring all the time. Return to saucepan and heat, stirring all the time, until thick. Simmer gently for 2–3 minutes. Remove from heat, add beaten egg yolks and mix well. Whisk egg whites and fold into cooked mixture. Pour into an ovenproof dish and bake at 160°C, 325°F, Gas Mark 3 for ½ hour or until golden brown on top.

APPLE CRISP

Serves 4

2 large cooking apples
2 oz. (*55g*) natural sultanas
   or raisins

Topping:
3 oz. (*85g*) milk-free
   margarine
3 oz. (*85g*) muscovado *or*
   demerara sugar
5 oz. (*140g*) porridge oats,
   millet flakes *or*
   buckwheat flakes

Peel and core apples, slice into a greased deep 8½" pie dish and add dried fruit.

Cream together the margarine and sugar and then work in the flakes. Spread over the apples. Bake at 180°C, 350°F, Gas Mark 4 for 45 minutes or until crisp and golden brown.
Serve hot or cold.

HONEYED APPLES

Serves 4

4 large cooking apples
4 tblspns. water

2 rounded tblspns. clear
   honey
Natural sultanas *or* raisins

Wash and core apples, score skin around middle with a knife. Place apples in an ovenproof dish and fill each one with sultanas or raisins. Add water to dish and spoon ½ tblspn. (½ x 15 ml) honey over each apple. Bake at 180°C, 350°F, Gas Mark 4 for 40–50 minutes, or until apples are tender.

BAKED APPLES

Serves 6

6 large cooking apples
6–8 oz. (*170–225g*) dates,
    finely chopped
1 lemon

3–4 oz. (*85–100g*) demerara
    sugar
2 oz. (*55g*) milk-free
    margarine
A few blanched almonds,
    shredded

Wash and core apples, score skin around middle with a knife, and place on a greased ovenproof dish. Stuff the dates into the cavities in the apples. Sprinkle apples with the finely grated rind and juice of the lemon and then with demerara sugar. Dot with a knob of milk-free margarine. Bake at 190°C, 375°F, Gas Mark 5 for 45–50 minutes or until apples are tender. Baste apples with juice from the base of the dish and scatter shredded almonds on the top. Return to oven for a further 5 minutes or until almonds are golden brown.
Serve hot.

CHOCOLATE OR CAROB SAUCE

1 oz. (*30g*) milk-free
    margarine
1 oz. (*30g*) cornflour *or*
    arrowroot
½ oz. (*15g*) raw cocoa
    powder *or* carob powder

1 oz. (*30g*) sugar *or* ½ oz.
    (*15g*) fructose
½ pt. (*250 ml*) goats' *or*
    sheep's milk

Mix flour and cocoa or carob with a little of the milk. Bring rest of milk to the boil and pour over mixture, stirring well. Return to heat to thicken. Add margarine and stir well until melted, and then sweeten to taste.
Serve with sponge pudding.

RUM AND RAISIN SAUCE

6 oz. (*170g*) natural raisins
3 tblspns. honey
Grated rind of 1 lemon
2 tblspns. lemon juice
Pinch of salt

1 tblspn. cornflour *or*
  arrowroot
8 fl.oz. (*225 ml*) water
2 tblspns. milk-free
  margarine
2 tblspns. rum

Combine the raisins, honey, lemon rind, lemon juice and salt. Blend the flour with the water and add to mixture. Bring to the boil, stirring gently, and then simmer for 4–5 minutes. Stir in the margarine and rum. May be reheated for later use.
Serve hot over puddings or pancakes.

SWEET ARROWROOT SAUCE

To use instead of custard.

1 tblspn. arrowroot
½ tblspn. sugar *or* 1 tspn.
  fructose

½ pt. (*250 ml*) goats', sheep's
  or soya milk

Put the arrowroot and sweetener of choice into a bowl or jug, add a little of the measured milk and mix well. Meanwhile, put rest of milk on to boil. Pour boiling milk over arrowroot, stirring all the time. Return mixture to saucepan and heat, stirring all the time, until thick. Simmer gently for 2–3 minutes.

SPICED ARROWROOT SAUCE

Follow the recipe and method for 'Sweet Arrowroot Sauce' adding 1 tblspn. lemon juice and a pinch of nutmeg *or* cinnamon to taste.

Starters and Soups

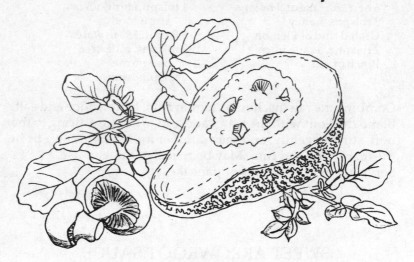

HUMMUS

Serves 6

A tasty 'dip' for parties. Serve with celery and carrot matchsticks or a choice of crispbreads which have been cut into fingers before baking.

8 oz. (225g) chick peas
2 garlic cloves, crushed
2 tblspns. oil
Juice of 1 large lemon

4 tblspns. natural goats' *or* sheep's yoghurt
Salt and pepper to taste
Chopped parsley to garnish
Paprika to garnish

Soak the chick peas overnight in sufficient water to cover well. Drain. Place in a saucepan with just enough water to cover. Add the garlic cloves and bring to the boil, cover and simmer for 30 minutes. Allow to cool in the water. Put oil, lemon juice and yoghurt into liquidiser. Add half the chick peas with the cooking liquor and garlic, and blend until smooth. Keep adding chick peas, along with some water if necessary, until they have all been incorporated. Season with salt and pepper to taste. Transfer to a serving dish, sprinkle with chopped parsley and paprika.

AVOCADO STARTER

Serves 2

1 avocado pear
4 oz. (110g) mushrooms
A small quantity of Soya
  Mayonnaise*

2 small sprigs of parsley
1 tblspn. oil of choice

Chop the mushrooms and saute them in the oil. Drain well and allow to cool. Put them together with a little soya mayonnaise into a bowl and mix well. You will need just enough mayonnaise to bind the mixture. Halve the avocado pear, peel and place each half on an individual dish. Pile mushroom mixture in the centres and garnish each with a sprig of parsley.
Serve immediately.

AVOCADO PATÉ

Serves 8

8 oz. (225g) soft goats'
  cheese *or* curd cheese*
1 large ripe avocado pear
Juice of ½ lemon

Salt and pepper to taste
Flavouring: nutmeg *or*
  parsley

Sieve the cheese into a bowl. Peel the avocado and remove the stone. Chop the flesh and blend in a liquidiser or food processor with the lemon juice, salt, pepper, cheese and either a pinch of nutmeg or a little chopped parsley. Spoon into serving dish and chill until required. Serve each portion on a small plate with a few sprigs of watercress or a leaf or two of lettuce.

Serve toast or crispbreads separately.

WATERCRESS AND CHEESE MOUSSE

Serves 3–4

4 oz. *(110g)* homemade
   sheep's curd cheese*
2 bunches watercress
4 tblspns. Mayonnaise*
4 tblspns. sheep's yoghurt

4 tblspns. vegetable stock
3 level tspns. gelatine
   (preservative-free) *or* 1½
   level tspns. agar agar
Salt and pepper to taste

Heat stock, dissolve gelatine or agar agar in it and then leave to cool. Wash the watercress well and trim off the coarse stems. Put into a food processor or liquidiser together with the cooled stock and blend to a fine purée. Season to taste. Put the curd cheese and mayonnaise into a large bowl and beat until smooth and then fold in the yoghurt. Finally, add the purée to the cheese mixture and fold gently together until well mixed. Pour into a wetted 1 pt. mould or into individual dishes and chill until set.

CUCUMBER AND CHEESE MOUSSE

Follow recipe and method for 'Watercress and Cheese Mousse' substituting 3 oz. *(85g)* cucumber, unpeeled and cut into dice, instead of watercress.

STUFFED BABY BEETS

Serves 4

Serve as a first course or as a side salad.

8 baby beetroots, cooked
4 oz. (*110g*) soft goats'
   cheese *or* curd cheese*
Chives

1–2 tblspns. goats' milk
Salt and pepper to taste
1 punnet Mustard and Cress

Peel the skin from each beetroot. Scoop out the centre of each beetroot, taking care not to break the flesh. Chop the scooped out flesh. Turn the cheese into a bowl, add chopped chives and blend in sufficient milk to make a smooth consistency. Add chopped beetroot and seasoning. Divide mixture between each baby beet, piling the mixture attractively on top. Top each with a sprinkling of chopped chives and serve on a bed of mustard and cress.

Alternative: Stuffed Cucumber and Stuffed Tomatoes can be made in the same way.

CHILLED CUCUMBER AND YOGHURT SOUP

Serves 4

A simple summer soup which requires no cooking.

12 oz. (*340g*) natural goats'
   yoghurt
6" piece of cucumber, grated
1 tblspn. natural raisins,
   finely chopped
8 walnut halves, finely
   chopped

2 spring onions, finely
   chopped
1 tblspn. fresh mint, finely
   chopped
4–6 tblspns. (*90–120 ml*)
   goats' milk
Salt and pepper to taste

Place yoghurt in a large bowl and stir in all the other ingredients. The amount of milk required will depend upon the thickness of the yoghurt. Chill for 1 hour. Stir. Put into individual soup bowls, and sprinkle with a little chopped mint or garnish each with a small sprig of mint.

Alternative: If you wish to use sheep's yoghurt and milk instead of goats', then use less yoghurt and more milk to obtain the correct consistency.

CHILLED CUCUMBER AND TOFU SOUP

Follow the recipe and method for 'Chilled Cucumber and Yoghurt Soup' substituting silken tofu for yoghurt and soya milk for goats' milk. You may need to add more soya milk to obtain the correct consistency.

CREAMY CARROT SOUP

Serves 2

This recipe shows how silken tofu can be used instead of cream.

8 oz. (*225g*) carrots
4 oz. (*110g*) leeks, white part
　　only
½ pt. (*250 ml*) vegetable
　　stock

5 fl.oz. (*125 ml*) silken tofu
½ tspn. ground mace
Salt and pepper to taste

Scrub carrots and cut into slices and put into a pan together with shredded leeks. Cover with vegetable stock and simmer until completely tender. Allow to cool. Liquidise to a purée and if you want the soup to be smooth rub through a fine sieve. Stir in the silken tofu and season to taste.

Chill if it is to be served cold or, if serving hot, heat through gently but do not allow to boil.

CREAMY TURNIP SOUP

Follow recipe and method for 'Creamy Carrot Soup' substituting turnips for carrots.

POLISH BEETROOT SOUP

Serves 3

1 medium onion
1 large carrot
1 lb. (*450g*) raw beetroot
½ tblspn. fresh parsley,
    chopped

1 bay leaf
Seasoning to taste
2 pts. (*1.2 l*) vegetable stock
1 egg white
Juice of ½ lemon

Peel and grate onion, carrot and beetroot. Put into large pan with parsley, bay leaf and stock. Simmer gently for 30 minutes. Pour through a sieve. Return to pan, whisk in 1 egg white and simmer gently for a further 15 minutes. Strain again. Stir in lemon juice and season to taste. Serve hot.

NOODLE SOUP

2½ pt. (*1.5 l*) vegetable stock
2 oz. (*55g*) carrot
2 oz. (*55g*) turnip
½ bunch of watercress *or*
    2 oz. (*55g*) spinach
2 oz. (*55g*) marrow *or*
    courgette, deseeded

2 oz. (*55g*) cucumber,
    deseeded
¼ cauliflower *or* some
    broccoli spears
1 oz. (*30g*) Japanese rice
    noodles

Wash all the vegetables. Cut carrot and turnip into ¼" dice or neat shapes. Trim the coarser stems from watercress or spinach, and wash well. Peel marrow and cut into small pieces. Cut courgette and cucumber into small pieces without peeling. Break cauliflower or broccoli into tiny florets. Heat stock in a large saucepan and cook carrot and turnip for about 10 minutes. Add rest of ingredients, except the noodles, and continue to cook until vegetables are tender. Prepare the rice noodles as directed on the packet and stir into the soup just before serving. Season to taste.

FLAKED RICE AND TOMATO SOUP

2 oz. (55g) brown rice flakes
2 oz. (55g) onion, chopped
1 tblspn. celery, chopped
½ oz. (15g) milk-free
   margarine
1 lb. (450g) tomatoes,
   skinned and chopped

½ bay leaf
½ tspn. ground mace
¾ tspn. marjoram or basil
1 pt. (500 ml) vegetable stock
Salt and pepper to taste
¼ pt. (125 ml) goats' or
   sheep's milk

Fry the onion and celery lightly in the margarine until soft and transparent. Add all the rest of the ingredients, except the milk, and simmer for 45 minutes. Remove the bay leaf. Rub through a sieve or blend in a liquidiser. Return to the pan together with the milk and reheat gently but do not allow to boil.

QUICK SCOTCH BROTH

Serves 4–6

3 oz. (85g) carrots
3 oz. (85g) turnip
3 oz. (85g) swede

1 leek or small onion
2 tblspns. barley flakes
2 pts. (1 l) vegetable stock
Seasoning to taste

Cut root vegetables into small dice, slice leek or chop onion. Add to saucepan together with flakes and stock. Bring to the boil, skim and simmer for 1 hour. Season to taste and serve.

CREAM OF CHESTNUT SOUP

Serves 3

8 oz. (*225g*) kibbled
   chestnuts
1 small onion *or* leek
1 carrot
1 stick of celery

1 tblspn. oil of choice
1½ pts. (*750 ml*) vegetable
   stock
Salt and pepper to taste

Wash and chop leek or peel and chop onion, carrot and celery. Heat oil in saucepan and sauté the chopped vegetables. Add kibbled chestnuts and stock and simmer gently for 1 hour. Purée in a liquidiser or by rubbing through a sieve. Return to pan and add salt and pepper to taste. Reheat gently but do not allow to boil.

GREEN PEA SOUP

Serves 4–6

8 oz. (*225g*) green split peas
2 pt. (*1.2 l*) water
2 vegetable stock cubes
1 large onion *or* 2 leeks,
   chopped

1 tblspn. oil of choice
¼–½ tspn. celery salt
Salt and pepper to taste

Wash the peas well and then soak overnight. Drain. Heat oil in a saucepan and sauté the onion or leeks until transparent.

Add the drained peas, measured water and stock cubes. Stir until the stock cubes have dissolved, then simmer for 1 hour. Season with celery salt, salt and pepper to taste. Allow to cool a little and then liquidise until smooth. Reheat gently before serving.

This makes a creamy textured soup. If you want a really thick soup then add a large scrubbed and chopped potato with the rest of the ingredients.

YELLOW PEA SOUP

Serves 4–6

8 oz. (*225g*) yellow split peas
8 oz. (*225g*) potatoes,
   scrubbed and cut up
1 tspn. muscovado sugar
Salt to taste
Mint, finely chopped
1 small carrot, chopped

1 small onion, chopped
1 garlic clove (optional)
½ pt. (*250 ml*) goats', sheep's
   or soya milk
1½ pt. (*750 ml*) water *or*
   vegetable stock

Wash peas well, discarding dark ones which float. Soak overnight. Drain. Put in pan and cover with fresh water and simmer for about 1¾–2 hours, adding more water as it boils away. Now add potatoes, onion, carrot, clove and sugar and continue simmering till all are soft, which will be about 15 minutes. Remove clove. Rub through a sieve or liquidise. Return to pan, add milk and salt and reheat gently but do not allow to boil. Serve sprinkled with chopped mint.

HARICOT BEAN SOUP

Serves 6

8 oz. (*225g*) haricot beans
1 large onion *or* 2 leeks
1 medium sized carrot
1 oz. (*30g*) margarine *or*
   vegetable fat
1½ pt. (*750 ml*) vegetable
   stock

2 garlic cloves, crushed
2 tblspn. tomato purée
1 tspn. yeast *or* vegetable
   extract
Salt and pepper to taste
Chopped parsley to garnish

Wash beans and soak overnight. Drain. Chop onion or leek and dice the carrots. Melt the fat and sauté the vegetables until onions are transparent. Put the drained beans into the pan with all the rest of the ingredients except the parsley. Simmer for 1 hour or until the beans are tender. Adjust seasoning to taste. Sprinkle with parsley.

Vegetables, Hot and Cold Savoury Dishes

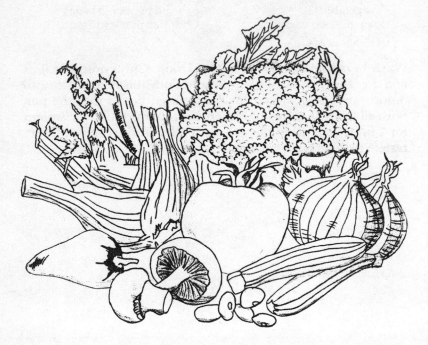

GLAZED SWEDE

An unusual and tasty way of serving a very common vegetable.

1–1½ lb. (450–675g) swede
Fat *or* oil for frying
Salt and black pepper

¼ tspn. ground nutmeg
2 oz. (55g) demerara sugar

Peel swede and cut into cubes. Cook in salted water for 10 minutes and then drain well. Put oil, seasoning, nutmeg and sugar into frying pan and heat. Add drained swede and fry over medium heat for 15 minutes or until swedes are golden brown and tender. Serve at once.

MAPLED PARSNIPS

Serves 4

8 small parsnips, trimmed
   and peeled
2–3 tblspns. maple syrup
1½ tblspns. milk-free
   margarine

2 tspns. lemon juice
¼ tspn. grated lemon rind

Put parsnips into a heavy based saucepan with ½" of boiling water, cover and cook for 4–5 minutes. Remove from heat, drain well. Combine remaining ingredients in same pan and heat over medium heat to simmering point. Return parsnips to pan and cook, uncovered, turning frequently, until parsnips have absorbed all the glaze (about 4 minutes). Serve immediately.

CABBAGE TOSS

1 large onion
4 oz. (*110g*) carrots
2 oz. (*55g*) milk-free
   margarine *or* 2 tblspns.
   olive oil

1½ lb. (*675g*) cabbage
1½ oz. (*45g*) natural sultanas
Salt and pepper to taste

Peel and chop onion. Peel carrots and cut into matchsticks. Put margarine or oil into a large frying pan with a lid and heat.

Add the onion and carrot to pan and cook slowly without browning for 5 minutes. Shred the cabbage finely and add to the pan. Toss the ingredients together in the pan, add seasoning, cover and cook gently for 15–20 minutes, turning occasionally. Remove from heat and add sultanas, mixing in well. Transfer to warmed serving dish.

SWEET POTATO MARIE

1 lb. (*450g*) sweet potatoes   Milk-free margarine
Salt and pepper to taste

Wash potatoes and boil in salted water until tender. Drain and peel when cooled. Mash with salt and pepper and milk-free margarine. Put into a small oven-proof dish and dot with milk-free margarine. Put under a hot grill until golden or bake at 180°C, 350°F, Gas Mark 4 until golden.

PEASE PUDDING

Serves 4–6

This dish is traditionally made with yellow split peas; however, green split peas would be equally good.

1 lb. (*450g*) split peas   Yolk of 1 standard egg
½ level tspn. salt   Salt and pepper to taste
½ oz. (*15g*) milk-free
  margarine

Soak the peas overnight. Drain. Put into a saucepan and cover with fresh water. Add salt and bring slowly to the boil. Cover and simmer gently for 2 hours, stirring occasionally. Add a little extra boiling water if peas begin to get too dry. Rub through a sieve or purée in a liquidiser. Add margarine and egg yolk. Mix well. Season to taste. Transfer to a 1 pt. greased ovenproof dish and bake at 180°C, 350°F, Gas Mark 4 for 30 minutes.

HARICOT BEANS

Serves 4

8 oz. (225g) haricot beans
Salt and pepper to taste

Knob of milk-free
margarine
Chopped parsley

Soak the beans overnight and then drain off the water. Put into a saucepan and cover with fresh water. Bring to the boil and then simmer gently for 45–50 minutes or until beans are tender but not mushy. Add salt after ½ hour. Drain the beans well and season to taste. Serve topped with a knob of milk-free margarine and sprinkled with chopped parsley.

BAKED BEANS

Serves 4

8 oz. (225g) haricot beans
1 lb. (450g) ripe tomatoes

Salt and pepper to taste
A little chopped onion

Soak the beans overnight and then drain off the water. Place the tomatoes in a bowl and pour boiling water over them, leave for a minute or two and then skin the tomatoes. Remove seeds, if desired. Put into a casserole dish together with the rest of the ingredients and cover. Bake at 190°C, 375°F, Gas Mark 5 for 2¼ hours or until beans are tender. Check after first hour and if mixture is not moist enough add some boiling water.

COURGETTES PROVENÇALE

Serves 3

1½ lb. (*675g*) courgettes
1 small onion (optional)
3 tblspns. olive oil
8 oz. (*225g*) tomatoes
Salt and pepper

1 level tblspn. fresh basil, chopped *or* 1 level tspn. dried basil
2 oz. (*55g*) grated vegetable rennet cheese

Wash the courgettes, cut into ½" slices, discarding the ends. Peel and chop onion. Heat oil in a saucepan and add courgettes and onion. Cook for 8–10 minutes or until just tender, stirring occasionally. Drain and arrange in overlapping circles in a small ovenproof dish. Slice washed tomatoes and fry for a few minutes, but do not allow to go soft. Add salt, pepper and basil. Arrange in one overlapping circle over courgettes. Sprinkle with grated cheese and bake at 190°C, 375°F, Gas Mark 5 for 25 minutes until golden brown.

SALSIFY (OR SCORZONERA) AU GRATIN

1 lb. (*450g*) young salsify *or* scorzonera roots
Salt
½ pt. (*250 ml*) goats' *or* sheep's milk
1 tblspn. arrowroot *or* cornflour

Pinch of nutmeg, paprika, cayenne *or* chilli powder
3 large tomatoes *or* mushrooms
4 oz. (*110g*) grated vegetable rennet cheese

Scrub the salsify (or scorzonera) thoroughly. Cook in boiling salted water for 40–45 minutes until tender. Drain thoroughly, peel the skins off and put the roots into an oiled ovenproof dish. Mix the arrowroot or cornflour with a little of the measured milk. Bring the rest of the milk to the boil. Pour over mixed flour, stirring well, and return to the pan. Bring back to the boil and cook for 2–3 minutes. Add seasoning of choice.

Skin, seed and chop the tomatoes or peel and chop the mushrooms; add to the sauce with half of the cheese. Spoon over the vegetable and sprinkle with remaining cheese. Either brown under the grill or bake at 190°C, 375°F, Gas Mark 5 for 15 minutes.

STUFFED PEPPERS

Serves 3

3 large even-sized peppers
2–3 tblspns. oil of choice
1 small chopped onion
2 oz. (*55g*) button
 mushrooms
4 oz. (*110g*) long-grain
 brown rice

½ pt. (*250 ml*) vegetable
 stock
2–3 tomatoes
1 tblspn. fresh parsley,
 chopped
Salt and pepper to taste
3 sprigs of parsley to garnish

Heat oil in pan and fry onion until soft. Add mushrooms and rice and cook gently for 1–2 minutes. Add stock and simmer, covered, until rice is tender and most of the liquid has been absorbed. Add chopped skinned tomatoes and parsley. Season to taste. Cut a slice off the top of each pepper at stalk end. Scoop out seeds and pith. Place in a large pan of boiling water and leave for 2–3 minutes to blanch. Lift out and drain. Brush outsides with a little oil and set on an ovenproof dish. Divide filling into three and fill each pepper. Cover with kitchen foil or a lid and bake at 190°C, 375°F, Gas Mark 5 for 20 minutes.

STUFFED AUBERGINES

Serves 4

4 medium-sized aubergines
4 large tomatoes
1 medium-sized onion
1 oz. (*30g*) milk-free
    margarine

2 oz. (*55g*) breadcrumbs
    (any type of flour) *or*
    freshly cooked long-
    grain brown rice
4 oz. (*110g*) vegetable rennet
    cheese
½ level tspn. salt
Black pepper

Remove stalks from aubergines, place in a large saucepan and cover with water. Bring to the boil, cover, and simmer for 15 minutes. Drain. Cut aubergines in half lengthwise. Scoop out flesh and chop. Place aubergine shells in a shallow ovenproof dish. Put tomatoes in a bowl and cover with boiling water. Leave for 1 minute, drain, skin and chop. Peel and chop onion finely. Melt margarine in frying pan and add chopped onion and aubergine. Fry for 5 minutes and then stir in chopped tomatoes and continue to fry gently for a minute or so. Remove from heat. Cut cheese into ½" cubes and add to mixture with the rest of the ingredients. Fill aubergine shells and cook in centre of oven at 180°C, 350°F, Gas Mark 4 for 30–40 minutes or until tender and golden.

GLAZED ONIONS WITH MAIZE STUFFING

1½ cups Maizemeal
    Breadcrumbs*
2 Spanish onions (about
    12 oz. each)
4 tblspns. milk-free
    margarine
10 tblspns. maple syrup

¼ pt. (*125 ml*) vegetable
    stock
2 sticks celery with leaves
2 oz. (*55g*) natural raisins *or*
    sultanas
Salt and black pepper to
    taste

Spread maizemeal breadcrumbs on a baking tray and pop in a warm oven to dry out while you prepare the other ingredients.

Lightly grease an ovenproof dish. Peel onions and cut in half crosswise. Scoop out onion centres with melon baller or spoon, being careful to leave the shells with ¼" at the sides and ½" at the base. Reserve remaining centres for the stuffing. Place the onion shells in prepared ovenproof dish. Smear the shells, inside and out, with half of the margarine. Spoon 2 tblspns. (*30 ml*) maple syrup into each shell and pour half the vegetable stock into the bottom of the dish and cover with a lid. Bake at 180°C, 350°F, Gas Mark 4 for 15 minutes. Uncover and baste upper edges with maple syrup in cavities. Continue baking uncovered until tender, about a further 15 minutes.

To make the stuffing: Heat the remaining margarine in the frying pan and sauté chopped onion for 1 minute. Chop celery finely and add to onion and continue to sauté until vegetables are soft. Stir in the sultanas or raisins. Remove from heat and add maizemeal breadcrumbs and then stir in sufficient vegetable stock to hold stuffing together when scooped with a spoon. Season to taste. Mould stuffing into 4 balls and mould into onion cavities. Baste with liquid from base of dish and bake for a further 15 minutes.

Alternative: Millet Batter Bread or Sorghum Batter Bread may be substituted for Maizemeal Bread, however the filling will lose its golden colour.

STUFFINGS

Most stuffing recipes call for breadcrumbs, however, they are equally good made with rice. Use the same quantity of long-grain brown rice as breadcrumbs. Simmer the rice until just tender and drain well. Do not overcook the rice or it will make the stuffing mushy. Add the rest of the ingredients to the drained cooked rice and use in the usual way.

MILD CHESTNUT STUFFING

4 oz. (*110g*) Potato and
   Chestnut Bread* *or* Rice
   and Chestnut Bread*
1 oz. (*30g*) milk-free
   margarine

Finely chopped herbs to
   taste
2 tblspns. water or stock
Salt and pepper

Make the bread into breadcrumbs. Melt the margarine and
add together with rest of ingredients to the breadcrumbs. Mix
well and put on a small greased baking tray or ovenproof dish
and bake in a hot oven for about 20 minutes.

CHESTNUT STUFFING

4 oz. (*110g*) kibbled
   chestnuts
8 oz. (*225g*) pearl *or* very
   small onions
2 tblspns. milk-free
   margarine
1 small apple, peeled, cored
   and diced

2 cloves garlic, crushed
6 tblspns. maple syrup
½ tspn. orange zest, finely
   grated
½ tspn. fresh root ginger,
   finely grated
Freshly ground pepper

Soak the chestnuts in water to cover overnight. Drain and
place in small saucepan with fresh water to cover by 2″.
Simmer, uncovered, for 1 hour. Drain chestnuts.

Cut an 'x' in the root end of each onion with tip of paring
knife. Blanch onions in small saucepanful of boiling water for
1 minute. Drain onions, then cut off roots and slip off outer
skins. Melt milk-free margarine in frying pan and sauté
onions, shaking pan frequently, until onions are browned on
all sides, about 5 minutes. Reduce heat and add diced apple
and drained chestnuts. Sauté, stirring until apple is browned,
about 1 minute. Add garlic and stir in maple syrup, orange
zest and ginger. Simmer mixture, uncovered, for about 1
minute until syrup thickens. Remove from heat, season to
taste and use in the usual way.

NUTTY PILAFF

Serves 6

1 small onion
3 oz. (85g) milk-free
  margarine
12 oz. (340g) long-grain
  brown rice, washed
1½ pts. (750 ml) vegetable
  stock
Pinch of turmeric *or* saffron
  powder
2 oz. (55g) natural sultanas

2 oz. (55g) natural raisins
1 bay leaf
Salt and pepper
3–4 oz. (85–110g) blanched
  almonds *or* cashews
6 hard-boiled eggs
Paprika for garnish
Chopped parsley for
  garnish

Peel, slice and finely chop onion. Fry in 2 oz. (55g) of the milk-free margarine until tender, but not brown. Stir rice into pan and cook for 1 minute. Gradually add stock, turmeric or saffron powder, sultanas, raisins, bay leaf and seasoning. Cover pan and simmer for 30–35 minutes, stirring occasionally, until rice is tender. Stir in shredded nuts and remaining 1 oz. (30g) milk-free margarine and cook for a further 2 minutes. Adjust seasoning, if necessary. Shell hard-boiled eggs and cut in half lengthwise. Pile pilaff onto a warmed serving dish. Place egg halves around the edge and sprinkle each egg with paprika. Sprinkle the pilaff with chopped parsley. Serve with salad.

OATMEAL AND CHEESE ROAST

1 large onion *or* leek, finely
  chopped
2 oz. (55g) milk-free
  margarine *or* 2 tblspns.
  oil of choice
3 oz. (85g) medium oatmeal
4 oz. (110g) vegetable rennet
  cheese, grated

¼ pt. (125 ml) vegetable
  stock
1 rounded tspn. yeast *or*
  vegetable extract
1 egg, beaten
Seasoning to taste

Fry the onion or leek in the margarine or oil until soft but not brown. Add the oatmeal and stock and cook over a low heat for 15 minutes, stirring from time to time. The mixture should then be fairly stiff. Remove from the heat, add the rest of the ingredients and mix well. Turn into a greased or oiled ovenproof dish and bake at 180°C, 350°F, Gas Mark 4 for 30 minutes. Cauliflower makes a good accompaniment.

MILLET CROQUETTES

8 oz. (*225g*) millet flakes
1 pt. (*500 ml*) water
Salt and pepper to taste
2–3 tblspns. vegetable rennet cheese, grated

1 onion, finely chopped and fried
Parsley to taste
2 eggs, beaten

Combine millet flakes with water and simmer gently, stirring continuously until thick. Remove from the heat and leave in pan until cool. Mix in the fried onion, parsley, beaten eggs and grated cheese. Shape into rolls and fry in hot fat or oil until golden brown.

MILLET OMELETTE

8 oz. (*225g*) millet flakes
½ pt. (*250 ml*) lukewarm goats', sheep's *or* soya milk
Pinch of dried herbs (optional)

3 eggs
1–2 rounded tspns. yeast *or* vegetable extract

Dissolve extract in milk, add millet flakes and then rest of ingredients. Beat well, and leave to stand for ½ hour. Fry on both sides in frying pan with the lid on. Serve plain or filled as desired.

MILLET OR SORGHUM CASSEROLE

7 oz. (*200g*) whole millet *or* sorghum
2 tblspns. (*30 ml*) olive oil
1 chopped onion *or* leek
2 chopped *or* sliced carrots
½ tspn. salt

5 fl.oz. (*125 ml*) goats' *or* sheep's yoghurt
6 oz. (*170g*) sliced mushrooms
1–2 tblspns. Epicure vegetable purée
2 pts. (*1 l*) water
Black pepper, to taste

Lightly brown the millet or sorghum in heavy pan over low heat, then remove the millet or sorghum from the pan. Fry the onion or leek in the oil until just coloured. Add the browned millet or sorghum, carrots, salt and pepper. Dissolve the vegetable purée in the water, add to the pan and bring to the boil, cover and bake at 180°C, 350°F, Gas Mark 4 for 1 hour. Add the mushrooms and cook for a further 1½ hours, checking to see that it does not boil dry.

Stir in the yoghurt and heat gently but do not boil. Serve immediately

CARROT AND CHEESE SAVOURY

1 large onion, grated
¼ pt. (*125 ml*) goats' *or* sheep's milk
3 oz. (*85g*) vegetable rennet cheese, grated
2 oz. (*55g*) milk-free margarine

4 oz. (*110g*) porridge oats, buckwheat flakes *or* millet flakes
2 large carrots, grated
½ tspn. basil *or* oregano
Salt and pepper to taste

Mix together grated carrot and onion. In a separate bowl mix together flakes, cheese, herb of choice and seasoning. Grease or oil a deep ovenproof dish. Arrange alternate layers of the two mixtures in the dish, starting and finishing with the cheese mixture. Pour milk over and dot with margarine. Place high up in oven and bake at 200°C, 400°F, Gas Mark 6 for about 30 minutes or until golden brown. Serve hot or cold with green salad.

LENTIL ROAST

8 oz. (*225g*) green lentils
2 oz. (*55g*) milk-free
    margarine *or* vegetable
    fat
1 onion *or* leek, chopped
2 large tomatoes, skinned *or*
    2 courgettes, sliced
2 oz. (*55g*) breadcrumbs, any
    type

1 small peeled, cored and
    chopped apple *or*
    1 carrot, grated
1 tspn. fresh thyme,
    chopped
2 tspns. fresh parsley,
    chopped
Salt and pepper to taste

Soak the lentils overnight in cold water. Drain. Put them into saucepan and cover with fresh water. Bring to the boil and simmer gently until they are soft and all the water has been absorbed. Mash them well with a potato masher.

Heat the fat and fry the onion or leek, vegetables and fruit until quite soft. Add the lentils, together with the breadcrumbs, herbs and season to taste.* Press into a greased basin or Pyrex bowl. Cover with greased paper or foil and bake at 190°C, 375°F, Gas Mark 5 for 1 hour.

Variations: Haricot beans or dried peas can be used instead of lentils.

This mixture can be used for croquettes, rissoles, burgers, 'sausage roll' filling or pies and pasties. Follow instructions down to * and then proceed accordingly.

HARICOT BEAN SAVOURY

12 oz. (*340g*) haricot beans
1 level tspn. salt
8 oz. (*225g*) skinned
    tomatoes

1 med. sized onion
3 oz. (*85g*) vegetable rennet
    cheese, grated

Soak beans overnight and drain. Transfer to saucepan and cover with fresh water. Bring slowly to the boil, cover and simmer until tender or for 1¾–2 hours. Finely chop the tomatoes or pulp them. Combine with drained cooked beans. Transfer to a 2 pt. *(1 l)* heatproof dish. Sprinkle with the grated cheese. Bake towards top of oven at 190°C, 375°F, Gas Mark 5 for 30 minutes.

LEEK AND HARICOT BEAN SAVOURY

Serves 4

8 oz. *(225g)* haricot beans
1 lb. *(450g)* leeks
8 oz. *(225g)* mushrooms
1½ oz. *(45g)* milk-free margarine
1 oz. *(30g)* soya flour
½ pt. *(250 ml)* goats', sheep's or soya milk

¼ tspn. yeast *or* vegetable extract
Black pepper
8–9 oz. *(225–255g)* Gluten-free spaghetti *or* Soba (Buckwheat Spaghetti)

Soak the beans overnight. Drain and place them in a pan of cold water, bring to the boil and cook for 50–60 minutes or until tender. Drain and set aside. Trim the leeks and cut diagonally into ½″ slices. Place ½ pt. *(250 ml)* cold water in a pan and bring to the boil. Add the leeks and cook until only just tender. Drain, reserving the liquid.

Put the spaghetti on to cook according to the instructions on the pack.

Wipe and slice the mushrooms. Melt the margarine in a pan and sauté the mushrooms for 2–3 minutes. Stir in the soya flour and cook, stirring continuously, for 1 minute. Remove from the heat and gradually blend in the milk. Add the yeast or vegetable extract with enough of the liquid reserved from the leeks to make a sauce. Stir in the cooked beans and leeks and season to taste with black pepper. Heat through gently. Serve the cooked spaghetti in a ring on each plate and pour the bean and leek sauce into the centre.

GLUTEN-FREE MACARONI CHEESE

Serves 4

5 oz. (*140g*) gluten-free
   macaroni
2 level tblspns. (*30 ml*)
   cornflour
1 pt. (*500 ml*) goats' *or*
   sheep's milk

7 oz. (*200g*) grated vegetable
   rennet Cheddar *or* hard
   sheep's cheese
Salt and pepper
¼ tspn. Grey Poupon Dijon
   Mustard *or* homemade
   Mustard*

Cook the macaroni in boiling water, as directed on packet. Drain. Mix the cornflour with 2 tblspns. of the measured milk. Pour the rest of the milk into a saucepan and bring to the boil. Pour over the cornflour mixture and stir very well. Return to pan and bring back to the boil. Simmer for 3 minutes. Beat in mustard and seasoning. Stir in about three quarters of the cheese and add the cooked macaroni. Pour into an ovenproof dish and sprinkle with the rest of the cheese. Put under a hot grill until the top is golden brown.

GLUTEN-FREE SPAGHETTI SOUFFLÉ

3 oz. (*85g*) gluten-free
   spaghetti
1 oz. (*30g*) cornflour
½ pt. (*250 ml*) goats' *or*
   sheep's milk

4–5 oz. (*110–140g*) vegetable
   rennet cheese, grated
2 eggs
Chopped chives *or* spring
   onions
Seasoning to taste

Cook the spaghetti as directed on the pack and drain. Mix the cornflour with a little of the milk and bring the rest of the milk to nearly boiling point. Pour over the cornflour mixture, stirring well and return to pan. Heat gently and allow to

bubble for 2–3 minutes. Remove from the heat and stir in grated cheese, egg yolks, seasoning, chives and cooked spaghetti. Finally fold in stiffly beaten egg whites. Bake in a souffle dish for approx. 25 minutes at 200°C, 400°F, Gas Mark 6.
Serve hot.

SPAGHETTI NEOPOLITAN

Serves 2

2 tblspns. (*30 ml*) olive oil
1 onion, peeled and
   chopped
1 clove garlic, peeled and
   crushed
1 lb. (*450g*) tomatoes,
   skinned and deseeded
2 level tblspns. tomato
   purée
2 medium-sized courgettes,
   washed and sliced

4 oz. (*110g*) gluten-free
   spaghetti
1 level tspn. dried oregano
   or basil
Salt and pepper to taste
Garnish: grated vegetable
   rennet cheddar, hard
   goats' *or* sheep's cheese
   or parmesan

Heat oil in pan, add onion and garlic and fry gently to soften but not colour the onion. Add tomatoes, tomato purée and courgettes and cook for a further 10 minutes, stirring occasionally, adding a little water, as necessary, to prevent the mixture from becoming too dry.

Meanwhile, cook the spaghetti as directed on the packet.

When vegetable mixture is ready, stir in the herb of choice and season to taste.

Serve vegetable sauce on a bed of spaghetti and garnish with grated cheese of choice.

SOYA BOLOGNESE

To serve with gluten-free spaghetti *or* buckwheat spaghetti.

4 oz. (*110g*) textured soya protein
1 tspn. oregano *or* marjoram
8 fl.oz. (*225 ml*) water
1 onion, chopped
1 clove garlic, crushed

1 tblspn. olive oil
1 lb. (*450g*) tomatoes, skinned, deseeded and chopped
1 tspn. yeast *or* vegetable extract
1 dessertspoonful tomato purée
Salt and pepper to taste

Simmer textured soya protein in the water for a few minutes. Fry onion and garlic in the oil and then add tomatoes and herbs. Continue to fry, stirring, for a further 5 minutes. Add textured soya protein, tomato purée and yeast or vegetable extract. Season to taste and cook for another 15 minutes.

Meanwhile, prepare the gluten-free spaghetti or buckwheat spaghetti according to the instructions on the pack. Serve each portion on a bed of spaghetti. Sprinkle with parmesan cheese, grated vegetable rennet cheese or chopped parsley according to taste.

SOYA SHEPHERD'S PIE

5 oz. (*140g*) textured soya protein
½ pt. (*250 ml*) water
1 medium onion, chopped
1 oz. (*30g*) milk-free margarine

1 tspn. yeast *or* vegetable extract
1 tblspn. Epicure Tomato, Mushroom *or* Vegetable Purée
2 tspns. mixed dried herbs
Mashed potato to cover

Simmer textured soya protein in the water to soften and then add seasoning and herbs. Lightly fry chopped onion in the margarine and add to the soya mixture along with all the rest of the ingredients, except the mashed potato. Continue to simmer gently until fairly firm but not dry. Place in a greased ovenproof dish and cover with mashed potato. Brown under a medium grill.

VEGETARIAN 'SAUSAGE' AND APPLE PIE

6 oz. (*170g*) brown rice flour
2 level tspns. wheat-free
   baking powder
Pinch of salt
3 oz. (*85g*) vegetable
   shortening
6 oz. (*170g*) sieved cooked
   potato
3 medium-sized cooking
   apples

1 tblspn. fresh parsley,
   chopped
8 oz. (*225g*) green lentils
2–4 tblspns. water
1 tspn. Epicure Vegetable
   Purée *or* Mushroom
   Purée
1 tblspn. onion, grated
Pinch of dried thyme
Salt and pepper to taste

Soak the lentils overnight in cold water. Drain. Put into saucepan and cover with fresh water. Bring to the boil and simmer until they are soft and the water has been absorbed. Mash until smooth and set aside.

Sieve flour, salt and baking powder into a bowl. Rub in the vegetable shortening until the mixture resembles fine breadcrumbs. Add sieved potato and mix in using the fingers to draw the mixture together, adding a little water if necessary. Knead lightly and set aside.

Peel, core and slice apples and mix with the chopped parsley. Arrange in base of greased 1½ pt. deep Pyrex pie plate. Mix the purée of choice with 2 tblspns. (*30 ml*) water and mix this with the prepared lentils to give a moist consistency, adding a little more water if necessary. Stir in the grated onion, thyme and seasoning. Spread lentil mixture over apples. Roll out the pie crust and lift gently into place, trim and knock up the edge. Bake at 200°C, 400°F, Gas Mark 6 for 25–30 minutes or until cooked and top is golden brown. Serve hot.

PIZZA

Makes 2

Dough:
Use 1 batch of either 'Mixed Flour Bread' or 'Potato and Rice Bread' recipe and add 1 level tspn. (*5 ml*) mixed dried herbs to the dough.

Topping:
1 lb. (*450g*) fresh tomatoes, skinned and chopped
Salt and pepper to taste
1 tspn. basil
4 oz. (*110g*) vegetable rennet cheese, grated

2 oz. (*55g*) mushrooms, sliced and sautéed
2–3 tblspns. olive oil
Black olives to garnish

Divide dough between two greased or oiled sandwich tins and bake at 180°C, 350°F, Gas Mark 4 for 20 minutes.

Mix together tomatoes, basil and seasoning. Spread tomato mixture onto part-baked dough, arrange sautéed mushroom slices over tomato mixture and sprinkle with olive oil. Cover with grated cheese and garnish with a few halved and stoned olives. Put back into the oven and bake for a further 10–15 minutes. Serve hot with salad.

PANCAKES

Pancakes can be made with any type of true flour, (a true flour is one which has been ground and is not a starch), any type of milk and egg or whole egg replacer. This makes them very versatile. See suggestions in section on Waffles, Drop Scones and Pancakes.

STUFFED SAVOURY PANCAKES

These recipes make sufficient filling for 6–8 pancakes.

1 small onion, chopped
2½ oz. (*70g*) milk-free
  margarine
2½ oz. (*70g*) flour (same as
  for pancakes)

1 pt. (*500 ml*) vegetable stock
10–12 oz. (*285–340g*) any
  cooked vegetables

Lightly fry chopped onion in margarine. Add flour, stirring well and cook for a minute. Remove from the heat, slowly stir in stock. Bring to boil, stirring, and cook for a minute or two. Add prepared vegetables and season to taste.

1 oz. (*30g*) milk-free
  margarine
1 crushed clove of garlic

4 oz. (*110g*) sliced courgettes
6 oz. (*170g*) sliced
  aubergines

Lightly fry the garlic, add the rest of vegetables and continue to fry gently until soft. Add to sauce as above and then season to taste.

MEXICAN CORN AND RYE TORTILLAS

4½ oz. (*125g*) maizemeal
4½ oz. (*125g*) rye flour
5 tblspns. corn oil

½ tspn. salt
8 fl.oz. (*225 ml*) water
  (approx.)

Mix flours and stir in the oil. Add water gradually until it forms a soft, slightly sticky dough. Knead well. Put in a bowl and cover for about ½ hour. Roll out walnut-sized pieces on a rye-floured surface into circles about 5" in diameter. Cook tortillas in an ungreased frying pan or on a griddle. Allow to cook until bubbles appear and then turn over and cook the other side. Once cooked, keep warm in a covered dish in the oven until you have cooked the whole batch.

These tortillas are a staple food in Mexico and Ecuador, where they are served with a casserole of beans and hot chilli peppers.

TOFU BURGERS

Serves 4

1 tspn. olive oil
6 oz. (*170g*) leeks
4 oz. (*110g*) carrots
4 oz. (*110g*) mushrooms
1 tspn. oregano
2 oz. (*55g*) buckwheat *or* millet flakes

8 oz. (*225g*) tofu, thoroughly mashed
2 tblspns. tahini
2 tblspns. tamari
Seasoning to taste
1½ oz. (*45g*) sesame seeds

Chop the leeks finely, coarsely grate the carrot and slice the mushrooms. Put the oil into a heavy based pan and heat. Add the prepared vegetables and sauté for about 8 minutes. Remove from the heat, add oregano, flakes, tofu, tahini, tamari and season with salt and pepper. Stir the mixture well and then leave to cool for a few minutes. Divide the mixture into 8 portions and mould each one into a ball. Roll each ball in sesame seeds until well covered, and then flatten each ball into a burger shape with a potato masher or the palm of the hand. Grill or fry for about 5 minutes on each side.

CURRY SAUCE

Serves 4

2 oz. (*55g*) milk-free margarine *or* 1½ fl.oz. (*40 ml*) oil of choice
1 large finely chopped onion
1 crushed clove of garlic
1½–2 level tblspns. wheat-free curry powder
½ pt. (*250 ml*) vegetable stock
1 level tblspn. flour of choice

2 cloves
1 level tblspn. Epicure tomato *or* mushroom purée
½ level tspn. ground ginger
2 level tblspn. sweet pickle *or* chutney
1 tblspn. lemon juice
1 tblspn. demerara sugar
2 level tspn. salt

Heat margarine or oil in pan and add onion and garlic. Fry gently until onion is transparent. Stir in curry powder, cloves, purée, ginger, sweet pickle or chutney, lemon juice, sugar and flour. (If, however, you are using a starch such as cornflour, mix with a little of the measured stock and add with the next ingredients.) Gradually stir in the stock. Slowly bring to the boil, stirring constantly. Lower heat, season to taste and cover pan. Simmer gently for ½–¾ hour.

Use this sauce in any of the following three ways or with your own choice of ingredients.

VEGETABLE CURRY

Serves 4

1 quantity Curry Sauce*   1 lb. (*450g*) diced mixed
                                                          vegetables

Add the diced mixed vegetables to the hot curry sauce and simmer for 15 minutes, or until the vegetables are tender. Serve on a bed of boiled long-grain brown rice.

NUT AND MACARONI CURRY

Serves 4

8–9 oz. (*225–255g*) gluten-   6 oz. (*170g*) cashews *or*
free macaroni   walnuts, coarsely
                                                        chopped
                                                  1 quantity Curry Sauce*

Cook the macaroni in boiling water, as directed on packet. Drain. Add with nuts to hot curry sauce and reheat gently. Pile onto warmed plates and serve with a side salad.

EGG AND MACARONI CURRY

Serves 4

8–9 oz. (225–255g) gluten-free macaroni

4 large chopped hard-boiled eggs
1 quantity Curry Sauce*

Cook the macaroni in boiling water, as directed on packet. Drain. Add with chopped eggs to hot curry sauce and reheat gently. Pile onto warmed plates and serve with a side salad.

LENTIL CURRY

8 oz. (225g) lentils
2 oz. (55g) milk-free margarine *or* vegetable fat
2 large onions, chopped
1 tblspn. wheat-free curry powder

1 small peeled, cored and chopped apple
1 tspn. muscovado sugar
Good pinch of salt and pepper
Few drops of lemon juice

Soak lentils overnight. Drain. Put into a saucepan and cover with fresh water, then bring to the boil. Simmer gently until just soft but still whole. Fry the onion and apple in fat until onion is transparent. Mix in all the other ingredients and simmer gently for a few minutes.
Serve hot on a bed of boiled long-grain brown rice.

HARICOT BEAN CURRY

Follow recipe and method for 'Lentil Curry', substituting haricot beans for lentils.

CURRY SPECIAL

4 oz. (*110g*) desiccated coconut (preservative-free)
½ pt. (*250 ml*) goats' *or* sheep's milk
1 onion
1 clove garlic
1 oz. (*30g*) crystallised stem *or* root ginger
5 oz. (140g) milk-free margarine *or* 3 fl.oz. (*75 ml*) oil of choice

2 level tblspns. wheat-free curry powder
1½ oz. (*45g*) flour of choice
1 pt. (*500 ml*) vegetable stock
Salt and pepper
5 oz. (*140g*) natural goats' *or* sheep's yoghurt
1½ lb. (*675g*) diced mixed vegetables
3 tblspns. lemon juice

Bring coconut and milk to the boil and allow to simmer for 2 minutes. Strain the milk into a bowl and set aside to cool. Peel the onion and chop finely. Peel the clove of garlic and crush or chop very finely. Finely chop the ginger. Melt the margarine in a pan or add oil to the pan and fry prepared onion, garlic and ginger until the onion is tender and transparent. Sprinkle in the curry powder and flour and stir over gentle heat for 1–2 minutes. (If, however, you are using a starch such as cornflour, mix with a little of the measured stock and add with the next ingredients.) Gradually blend in the prepared coconut-flavoured milk, stock and seasoning. Bring to the boil and then simmer for 3–4 minutes, stirring constantly. Stir in the diced vegetables and cook gently for 15 minutes or so until the vegetables are tender. Blend in the lemon juice with a little of the curry sauce and then stir this into the pan. Stir in the yoghurt and reheat gently but do not boil. Serve at once with boiled long-grain brown rice and a selection of the following suggested accompaniments, each served in a separate dish.

ACCOMPANIMENTS FOR CURRY SPECIAL

Chutney or pickle, toasted chopped nuts, finely chopped crystallised or stem ginger, piccalilli,* mandarin oranges, crushed pineapple, sieved hard-boiled eggs, fried onion rings,* brandied raisins or sultanas,* poppadoms (gluten-free).
You will find recipes for gluten-free chutneys, pickles and piccalilli in this book.

FRIED ONION RINGS

Peel a large onion and cut into ¼" slices. Separate into rings. Dip into goats' or sheep's milk, drain slightly and then dip into seasoned flour of choice. Fry in deep hot fat or oil, cooking a few at a time, until golden and crisp. Drain well on crumpled kitchen paper. Keep hot.

BRANDIED RAISINS OR SULTANAS

4 oz. (*110g*) stoned *or*
seedless natural raisins
or natural sultanas

4 tblspns. brandy

Leave the fruit to soak in brandy for 3–4 hours or until well plumped up.

SWEETCORN AND TOFU FLAN

Serves 4

Line an 8″ flan tin with pastry of choice.

Filling:
1 tspn. oil of choice
4 oz. (*110g*) onion *or* leek
1 large garlic clove
5 oz. (*140g*) sweetcorn
 kernels

8 oz. (*225g*) tofu, thoroughly
 mashed
Salt and black pepper to
 taste

Cook the sweetcorn until tender and drain. Bake the pastry case 'blind' for 10 minutes, at 200°C, 400°F, Gas Mark 6. Chop onion or leek. Heat oil in a frying pan and cook onion or leek for about 7 minutes over gentle heat. Remove from heat, mix in tofu thoroughly, adding a little water to make a slightly soft consistency. Season with salt and black pepper to taste. Add cooked sweetcorn and stir well. Spoon into part-baked flan case and bake at 190°C, 375°F, Gas Mark 5 for 25 minutes.

WALNUT FLAN

Line an 8″ or 9″ flan tin with pastry of choice.

Filling:
12 oz. (*340g*) walnuts,
 ground
2 eggs, beaten
1 oz. (*30g*) milk-free
 margarine
2 oz. (*55g*) breadcrumbs, any
 type

1 tblspn. oil of choice
1 clove garlic, crushed
Pinch of dried thyme *or*
 basil
1 tspn. Epicure Tomato *or*
 Mushroom Purée
2 onions, chopped

Fry onion and garlic in oil until transparent. Add nuts, beaten eggs, herbs and flavouring. Mix well and then spoon mixture into the prepared flan case, sprinkling the breadcrumbs on the top. Dot with margarine. Bake at 200°C, 400°F, Gas Mark 6 for about 30 minutes. Serve hot with roast potatoes, vegetables and cranberry sauce or cold with salad.

SAVOURY MILLET BLANCMANGE

1 pt. (*500 ml*) goats', sheep's
   or soya milk
½ tspn. celery salt
1 tblspn. fresh parsley,
   chopped

Pinch of thyme
A little chopped chives
4 level tblspns. millet flakes
2 heaped tblspns. vegetable
   rennet cheese, grated

Put the milk, celery salt and flakes in a pan and bring to the boil. Boil for 10 minutes. Stir in the other ingredients and pour into a rinsed mould and leave to set.
Serve on a large dish surrounded by salad.

Note: The herbs and cheese are only a suggestion – you can use whatever you wish, i.e. mushrooms with oregano or tomato with basil.

SOYA SAVOURY LOAF

8 oz. (*225g*) textured soya
   protein
16 fl.oz. (*450 ml*) water
2 oz. (*55g*) breadcrumbs, any
   type
8 fl.oz. (*225 ml*) soya milk,
   unsweetened

2 eggs
1 tspn. yeast *or* vegetable
   extract
1 medium onion, chopped
A little oil of choice
¼ tspn. sage
Pinch of salt and pepper

Put textured soya protein and water into a saucepan and simmer to soften. Fry the chopped onion in the oil until transparent. Combine all the rest of the ingredients well and place in a greased or oiled ovenproof dish or bread tin. Bake at 180°C, 350°F, Gas Mark 4 for 1 hour. Serve hot or cold.

NUT LOAF

8 oz. (*225g*) any variety of nuts, ground
3 oz. (*85g*) breadcrumbs, any type
1 oz. (*30g*) flour, same as breadcrumbs
1 oz. (*30g*) porridge oats, buckwheat flakes *or* millet flakes

1 large onion
2 tomatoes *or* 2 oz. (*55g*) mushrooms
1 tblspn. oil of choice
¼ pt. (*125 ml*) vegetable stock
1 tspn. mixed dried herbs
A little yeast *or* vegetable extract

Chop onion and cook gently in oil for a few minutes. Skin, deseed and chop tomatoes or slice mushrooms and add to pan. Cook gently for a few minutes. Stir in the flour and then the stock. Stir well and simmer for about 2 minutes. Add all the rest of the ingredients and mix well. Put into a greased or oiled bread tin, cover with a piece of greaseproof paper and bake at 180°C, 350°F, Gas Mark 4 for about 30 minutes. Serve hot or cold with green salad.

VEGETABLE STOCK

A well-flavoured clear stock is a must for tasty meals but most stocks contain lactose, wheat or yeast which many cannot have. Of course, stock can be made at home but here are a number of suggestions, to save time, for products now available in some supermarkets and delicatessens as well as health shops.

Epicure   do a range of purées in tubes. As well as the old favourite tomato purée, there are now garlic purée, mushroom purée and vegetable purée. Ingredients for the vegetable purée are: tomato, carrot, vegetable oil, salt, onion, celery, basil and garlic.
A spoonful of any of these dissolved in water makes a good stock.

Campbells V-8   Tomato and Vegetable Juice. So called because it contains 8 vegetables. Ingredients: tomato, carrot, celery, beetroot, parsley, salt, lettuce, watercress, spinach and extract of spices. It comes in small cartons or large bottles like apple juice so look for it amongst the drinks and squashes. Makes a very pleasant drink or the basis for a tasty mixed vegetable soup. Also is ideal, diluted, for stock.

Morga Concentrated Vegetable Extract.   Ingredients: Sea salt, hydrolysed vegetable protein, hydrogenated vegetable fat, celery, onion, parsley, cabbage, carrots, leek, tomatoes, nutmeg, and garlic. Ideal for soups, gravies, stock and as a spread instead of yeast extract.

SAVOURY ASPIC

Use any of the above suggestions to make a well-flavoured stock as a basis for savoury aspic and you will have a tasty gel to make all sorts of moulds to serve with salad.

3 tspns. gelatine (preservative-free) *or* 1½ tspns. agar agar	2 tblspns. cider vinegar, brown rice vinegar *or* lemon juice
4 tblspns. hot water ½ pt. (*250 ml*) well-flavoured clear stock	Pinch of salt

Dissolve the gelatine or agar agar in hot water, add to stock. Add vinegar or lemon juice. Leave until just beginning to thicken and use as required.

TOMATO ASPIC

3 tspns. gelatine
    (preservative-free) *or*
1½ tspns. agar agar
¼ pt. (*125 ml*) hot water
½ pt. (*250 ml*) tomato juice
1 slice of onion
1 clove

½ tspn. salt
Pinch of pepper
1 tspn. sugar *or* ½ tspn.
    fructose
1 tblspn. cider vinegar,
    brown rice vinegar *or*
    lemon juice

Put the gelatine or agar agar in the hot water to dissolve. Add all flavourings to half of the tomato juice and cook until onion softens. Stir in the dissolved gelatine or agar agar and then add the rest of the ingredients. Strain and leave until just beginning to thicken and use as required.

MOULDED VEGETABLE SALAD

Choose a variety of vegetables of different colours. Here are some suggestions: cooked peas, cooked green beans, cubed celery, cooked cubed carrot, cubed cucumber, cubed cooked beetroot, small pieces of green or red pepper, finely chopped onion, asparagus tips, or sliced radishes.

1 quantity Savoury Aspic* *or*
    Tomato Aspic*

½ cup each of 4 or 5 different
    vegetables

Prepare aspic and let it cool. Pour a little into the bottom of a plain mould. When firm place pieces of vegetable onto the gel to form a pattern or design. Repeat the process also on each side of the mould, if wished. Leave to set. Fill mould with rest of vegetables and then carefully pour in rest of aspic. Put in refrigerator to set. Unmould onto a bed of lettuce.

SOYA AND NUT MOULDS

1 dessertspon. soya flour
½ pt. (*250 ml*) water
¼ pt. (*125 ml*) soya milk
4 oz. (*110g*) nuts of choice,
   ground *or* grated

4 level tspns. gelatine
   (preservative-free) *or*
   2 level tspns. agar agar
A little tamari

Whisk flour and water together and then bring to the boil.
Cook for a minute or two and then allow to cool. Dissolve the
gelatine or agar agar in a little hot water, then add the soya
milk and the soya flour mixture. Make up to 1 pt. (*500 ml*) with
cold water. Flavour with tamari and leave until just starting to
set. Stir in the prepared nuts and pour into wetted individual
moulds and leave to set. Turn out of moulds and serve on a
bed of salad.

Salads and Dressings

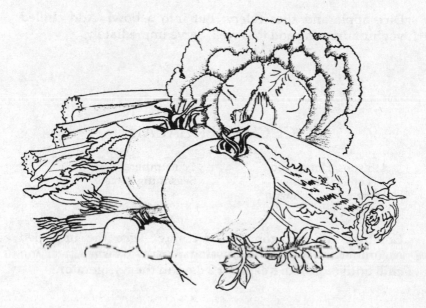

CARROT AND CELERIAC SALAD

8 oz. (225g) carrots
8 oz. (225g) celeriac

1 quantity Yoghurt
Dressing No. 1*, chilled
A little chopped parsley

Grate the carrot and celeriac into a bowl. Add chilled yoghurt dressing and toss well. Sprinkle with a little chopped parsley and serve immediately.

APPLE AND CELERY SALAD

2 Cox's Orange Pippins
1 head of celery

1 quantity Yoghurt
Dressing No. 1*, chilled

Dice apple and slice celery. Put into a bowl. Add chilled yoghurt dressing and toss well. Serve immediately.

CUCUMBER SALAD

4 tblspns. Honey and
   Lemon Dressing*
½ tspn. fresh tarragon,
   chopped

1 cucumber
Seasoning to taste

Combine the tarragon and dressing. Dice the unpeeled cucumber and toss in the dressing. Season to taste. Cover and chill until required. Keeps for 2 days in the refrigerator.

CREAMY BEETROOT SALAD

8 oz. (225g) raw beetroot

½ quantity Soya
   Mayonnaise*

Grate the raw beetroot and combine with the dressing. Chill and serve.

MUSTARD FAMILY SALAD

1 head of chinese leaves *or*
   ½ white cabbage
Bunch of watercress
Box of mustard and cress

Radishes
Tiny cauliflower florets
Mustard Mayonnaise*

Cut chinese leaves into 1″ strips or finely shred white cabbage. Wash and dry all the vegetables. Place chinese leaves or cabbage on serving dish and arrange mixture of watercress and mustard and cress over this. Slice radishes or cut into flowers. Garnish salad with radishes and cauliflower florets. Serve Mustard Mayonnaise in a separate bowl.

MIXED BEAN SALAD

Mix together a variety of dried beans of mixed colours and soak overnight. Rinse. Cook in fresh water until all varieties are tender. Drain and leave until completely cold. Toss with a little soya oil.

COCONUT COLESLAW

1 quantity Yoghurt
   Dressing, No. 1*
¼ tspn. paprika
¼ tspn. wheat-free curry
   powder

3 oz. (*85g*) desiccated
   coconut (preservative-
   free)
½ white cabbage, shredded
Spring onion for garnish

Soak coconut in yoghurt dressing for ½ hour. Add rest of ingredients and place in a serving dish. Garnish with chopped spring onions.

SWEET POTATO SALAD

8 oz. (225g) sweet potatoes	½ quantity Soya Mayonnaise*

Scrub the potatoes and cook in boiling salted water until just tender. Drain and leave until cold. Remove skins and dice the cold, cooked sweet potatoes and combine with the mayonnaise. Chill and serve.

TANGY PEPPER SALAD

1 medium-sized red pepper	4 tblspns. Honey and Lemon Dressing*
1 medium-sized green pepper	Lettuce
2 large oranges	

Arrange lettuce in the base of a serving dish. Shred the peppers, after removing the seeds and the pith. Cut the peel from the oranges, removing all the white pith and divide into segments by cutting each segment free from skin. Toss peppers and oranges with the Honey and Lemon Dressing and arrange on prepared bed of lettuce.

BELGIAN SALAD

Serves 4

A very attractive salad that looks like a giant sunflower.

1 large carrot	2 oz. (55g) shelled walnuts
2 heads chicory	Juice of ½ lemon
6 radishes	Salt and pepper to taste
1 eating apple	

Wash, scrape and grate carrot. Wash chicory, radishes and apple. Arrange chicory leaves around the edge of a large flat dish, radiating out from the centre. Slice any remaining chicory leaves. Trim and slice radishes. Cut walnuts into quarters. Cube apple. Place apple in a bowl and coat with lemon juice. Add all the rest of the sliced vegetables, walnuts and seasoning to taste. Mix and pile in centre of dish with the chicory leaves showing all the way round.

RUSSIAN SALAD

Serves 4

1 oz. (*110g*) cold cooked
   sliced green beans
6 oz. (*170g*) cold cooked
   whole potatoes
6 oz. (*170g*) cold cooked
   whole carrots
½ medium cold lightly
   cooked cauliflower

4 sticks celery
4 gherkins
1 tspn. fresh chives,
   chopped
Salt and pepper
½ pt. (*250 ml*) Soya
   Mayonnaise*

Dice potato and carrot. Cut cauliflower into small sprigs. Chop washed celery. Slice gherkins. Put all the vegetables into a large bowl and mix. Add half the chopped chives, seasoning and mayonnaise. Toss gently so as not to break the vegetables. Pile the Russian salad onto a bed of lettuce and top with remaining chopped chives.

PARSLEYED LEEKS AND MUSHROOMS

Serves 3–4

6 small leeks
Salt
4–6 oz. (*110–170g*) button
    mushrooms

Parsley dressing:
1 heaped tspn. sugar
Black pepper
Garlic salt
1 tblspn. cider vinegar *or*
    brown rice vinegar
4 tblspns. oil
2 level tblspns. fresh
    parsley, chopped

Trim outer leaves and end of stalks from leeks. Wash leeks well in plenty of water. Cut diagonally into 2" pieces with a sharp knife. Cook in boiling salted water for 8–10 minutes or until only just tender. Wash mushrooms and thinly slice. Lightly sauté the mushrooms in a little oil.

To make the parsley dressing:

Place the sugar, pepper and garlic salt to taste in a small bowl; add the vinegar and oil. Stir dressing well to mix and stir in chopped parsley. Lightly toss hot drained leeks and sliced mushrooms in prepared parsley dressing. Leave to cool, turning the ingredients occasionally. Serve cold.

CELERY BOATS

1 head of celery
Soft goats' cheese

Goats' milk

Cut required amount of washed celery into neat pieces. Put soft goats' cheese into a small basin and beat with a very little goat's milk until smooth. Fill celery pieces with the creamed cheese.

CHEESY PEACH SALAD

Serves 1

4 oz. *(110g)* soft goats'   1 fresh peach
   cheese

Place cheese on a dish. Peel, stone and slice the peach.
Garnish the cheese with peach slices. Serve immediately.

MELON SALAD

Serves 4

An unusual and refreshing summer salad.

½ large or 1 small honeydew   1 level tspn. Grey Poupon
   melon   Dijon Mustard *or*
2 oz. *(55g)* natural seedless   homemade Mustard*
   raisins   2 tblspns. natural goats' *or*
1 level tspn. spring onion,   sheep's yoghurt
   finely chopped   2 level tblspns. fresh
2 oz. *(55g)* flaked almonds   parsley, chopped
3 tblspns. French Dressing*

To Serve: Chinese leaves *or* cos lettuce

Cut the flesh out of the melon and dice. Place in a bowl with
raisins, spring onion and almonds. Blend dressing with
mustard, yoghurt and parsley. Pour dressing over melon
mixture and toss lightly. Serve on a bed of Chinese leaves or
cos lettuce.

FRENCH DRESSING

2 dessertspns. cider vinegar
  or brown rice vinegar
5 dessertspns. oil of choice

Pinch of salt
Seasoning

Put all ingredients into a screw-topped jar and shake well to blend.

HONEY AND LEMON DRESSING

1 tblspn. sunflower oil
1 tblspn. lemon juice

1 tblspn. clear honey

Put all ingredients into a screw-topped jar and shake well to blend.

YOGHURT DRESSING No.1

¼ pt. (*125 ml*) natural goats'
  or sheep's yoghurt
½ tspn. demerara sugar
1 tblspn. spring onion,
  chopped

Pinch of celery salt
Pinch of malic acid

Put all ingredients into a bowl and mix very well.

YOGHURT DRESSING No.2

¼ pt. (*125 ml*) natural goats'
  or sheep's yoghurt
½ tspn. clear honey

Juice and rind of ½ lemon
Pinch of either paprika,
  cayenne *or* chilli powder

Put all ingredients into a screw-topped jar and shake well to blend.

SALAD CREAM (EGG-FREE)

2 oz. (*55g*) milk-free
   margarine
2 level tspns. fructose
1 tspn. cider vinegar *or* rice
   vinegar

4 tspns. water
1 tspn. oil of choice
Squeeze of lemon juice *or*
   a pinch of malic acid
Salt and pepper to taste

Put margarine and fructose in a bowl and beat with a wooden spoon until creamy. Beat in vinegar of choice a little at a time and then do the same with the water and the oil. Finally beat in the lemon juice or malic acid and seasoning. Put in a jar with a wide neck and a screw top. Store in the refrigerator.

MAYONNAISE

1 egg yolk
1 tspn. honey
¼ tspn. salt

Juice of ½ lemon *or* ¼ level
   tspn. malic acid
½ pt. (*250 ml*) olive oil

Put egg yolk, honey, salt and lemon juice or malic acid into liquidiser goblet and blend briefly. Remove the porthole lid in the top of the liquidiser and gradually pour in oil, incorporating all the while, until the mayonnaise is the thickness desired. Put in a jar with a wide neck and a screw top. Store in the refrigerator.

SOYA MAYONNAISE

1 oz. (*30g*) soya flour
2 tblspns. (*30 ml*) water
8 fl.oz. (*225 ml*) soya oil

¼ tspn. salt
Juice of ½ lemon *or* ¼ level
tspn. malic acid

Make a smooth paste of soya flour and water in a bowl, standing in a pan of hot water, and let it heat. Slowly beat in oil with a rotary beater. Remove from heat when thick, season and add lemon juice or malic acid. Beat until smooth and thick. Put in a jar with a wide neck and a screw top. Store in the refrigerator.

MUSTARD MAYONNAISE

1 egg
½ tspn. salt
½ tspn. Dijon mustard *or*
homemade Mustard*

2 tspn. brown rice vinegar
½ pt. (*250 ml*) rapeseed *or*
corn oil

Break the egg into the liquidiser goblet. Add the salt, mustard and vinegar. Blend for 10 seconds. While the liquidiser is switched on, slowly pour in the oil through the port-hole in the lid. The mayonnaise will become thick as the oil if added.

To make the mayonnaise by hand: Beat the egg, salt, mustard and vinegar together with a wooden spoon. Add the oil a drop at a time until half of the oil has been used. Continue adding a little more at a time until all the rest of the oil has been blended in and the mayonnaise is thick and smooth.

Chutneys, Pickles, Mustards and Preserves

CHUTNEYS, PICKLES AND MUSTARD

Mustard powder is called for in many chutney and pickle recipes; however, it may well contain wheat. To overcome this, some of the recipes in this section include ground mustard seeds. Put the whole mustard seeds into a liquidiser or coffee grinder (sufficient to well cover the blades) and blend/grind to a fine powder. Store in a screw-topped jar if you do not require it all at once.

APPLE CHUTNEY

2 pts. (*1.2 l*) cider vinegar *or* brown rice vinegar
2 lb. (*900g*) apples, cored and peeled
1 lb. (*450g*) demerara sugar
1 lb. (*450g*) natural seedless raisins

1 lb. (*450g*) onions
1 oz. (*30g*) ground mustard seeds
1 tspn. cayenne pepper
2 tspns. salt

Chop apples, raisins (if large) and onion coarsely and mix with the other ingredients. Boil until the chopped ingredients are tender which will take about one hour. Pour into warm jars and seal in the usual way.

APRICOT CHUTNEY

2 lb. (*900g*) natural dried apricots
½ lb. (*225g*) onions
3 lb. (*1.350 kg*) demerara sugar
1 tspn. wheat-free curry powder

1 tspn. cinnamon
1 tspn. allspice
Pinch of cayenne pepper
2 pts. (*1.2 l*) cider vinegar *or* brown rice vinegar

Wash the apricots well, cover them with boiling water and leave for 24 hours. Chop onions and stew them with a little of the sugar until tender. Drain the apricots, cut into pieces and put back into the pan with the rest of the ingredients. Simmer until chutney is thick which will take about 2 hours. Pot and cover in the usual way.

TOMATO KETCHUP

1 pt. (*500 ml*) cider vinegar *or* brown rice vinegar
3 lb. (*1.350 kg*) ripe tomatoes
2 oz. (*55g*) salt
2 oz. (*55g*) demerara sugar
2 tspns. ground mustard seeds
1 tspn. white pepper

Put tomatoes into a large bowl and pour boiling water over them. Steep for a few minutes and then drain and peel. Chop them coarsely and sprinkle with salt. Leave for 3 hours. Add to pan with the rest of the ingredients and boil for ½ hour or until thick and smooth. Stir frequently while cooking to prevent mixture from sticking to the bottom of the pan. Pour into warm bottles while still hot and seal. When cold store in the refrigerator for short term use. If, however, you want to be able to store this ketchup for some time, it is necessary to sterilise the filled and sealed bottles in boiling water for ½ hour.

This can also be done in a pressure cooker by following the maker's instructions.

PRUNE CHUTNEY

An unusual chutney without onion or tomato.

1 lb. (*450g*) unsorbated prunes
¾ lb. (*350g*) apples
¼ lb. (*110g*) hazelnuts
½ pt. (*250 ml*) cider vinegar *or* brown rice vinegar
10 oz. (*285g*) muscovado sugar
½ tspn. wheat-free curry powder
½ tspn. cinnamon
¼ tspn. allspice
A pinch of cayenne pepper

Pour boiling water over the prunes and leave for 24 hours. Peel and core the apples, chop finely and stew until tender with a little of the sugar. Chop nuts finely. Remove prune stones, and cut prunes into pieces. Put vinegar of choice into a pan, add the sugar and mix in the remaining ingredients. Boil for ¾–1 hour, stirring frequently. Pot and cover at once.

MUSHROOM KETCHUP

Makes a good alternative to the more traditional tomato ketchup.

3 lb. (*1.350 kg*) mushrooms
2 oz. (*55g*) salt
1 pt. (*500 ml*) cider vinegar *or* brown rice vinegar
1 tspn. (*5 ml*) allspice
½ oz. (*15g*) fresh root ginger

1 blade of mace
6 cloves
½ stick of cinnamon
1 finely chopped onion
½ tspn. grated horseradish

Break the mushrooms into small pieces, sprinkle with salt and leave for 12 hours. Mash with a wooden spoon. Peel and coarsely chop fresh root ginger. Put all ingredients into a pan, cover and simmer for ½ hour. Strain through a fine sieve and pour into warm jars or bottles, leaving a 1½" gap at the top for expansion. When cold store in the refrigerator for short term use. If, however, you want to be able to store this ketchup for some time, it is necessary to sterilise the filled and sealed bottles in boiling water for ½ hour.

This can also be done in a pressure cooker by following the maker's instructions.

GREEN TOMATO CHUTNEY

2¼ pt. (*1.3 l*) cider vinegar *or* brown rice vinegar
4 lb. (*1.800 kg*) green tomatoes
1½ lb. (*675g*) onions
1½ lb. (*675g*) apples, peeled and cored
1 lb. (*450g*) natural sultanas

2 lb. (*900g*) demerara sugar
2 oz. (*55g*) ground mustard seeds
3 tspns. salt
1 oz. (*30g*) ground ginger
1 oz. (*30g*) crushed garlic
1 tspn. cayenne pepper
Juice of 2 lemons

Slice the apples, onions and green tomatoes thinly. Mix in the other ingredients thoroughly and simmer for about two hours, or until really thick. Pour into warm jars and seal in the usual way.

BENGAL CHUTNEY

3 pt. (*1.7 l*) cider vinegar *or* brown rice vinegar
1 lb. (*450g*) demerara sugar
2 oz. (*55g*) whole mustard seeds
8 oz. (*225g*) natural seedless raisins
2 oz. (*55g*) garlic

8 oz. (*225g*) onions
7 lb. (*3.150 kg*) cooking apples
1 tblspn. salt
½ oz. (*15g*) chilli powder
1 tspn. cumin powder
2 oz. (*55g*) fresh root ginger

Scrape the ginger and chop it with the onions and garlic. Add the cored, peeled and sliced apples. Simmer with the vinegar and sugar until apples are soft. Add the rest of the ingredients and simmer for a further 20 minutes, stirring frequently. Put into warm jars and seal in the usual way.

PICCALILLI

1 large cauliflower
2 cucumbers
2 lb. (*900g*) shallots *or* pickling onions
2 lb. (*900g*) apples
Brine
1 oz. (*30g*) chilli peppers
2 oz. (*55g*) garlic
1 oz. (*30g*) bruised root ginger

1 oz. (*30g*) black peppercorns
4 pts. (*2.2 l*) cider vinegar *or* brown rice vinegar
2 oz. (*55g*) tapioca flour *or* cornflour
1 oz. (*30g*) turmeric
1 oz. (*30g*) ground mustard seeds

Prepare all the vegetables and apples and cut into neat pieces. Cover with cold brine, leave overnight and then drain. Prepare the pickle sauce by boiling the chilli peppers, garlic, ginger and peppercorns in the vinegar for 5 minutes, and then pour in the tapioca flour or cornflour, turmeric and ground mustard seeds, which have previously been blended with a little cold vinegar. Stir and boil for 10 minutes to cook the starch. Pile the prepared vegetables into hot jars and pour over the pickling sauce. Cover and seal in the usual way.

MUSTARD

Dijon mustard is gluten-free but difficult to obtain. Here is a recipe to make your own mustard. The mustard seeds may be left whole or ground to a fine powder in the liquidiser depending upon whether you want the mustard to be smooth or not.

½ pt. (*250 ml*) cider vinegar *or* brown rice vinegar

2 oz. (*55g*) mustard seeds, whole *or* ground

1 oz. (*30g*) tapioca flour *or* cornflour

1 large pinch each of ground ginger, ground cloves, and ground caraway seeds

1 tspn. salt

2 oz. (*55g*) demerara sugar

Mix together the mustard, tapioca/cornflour, spices, salt and sugar. Blend in the vinegar and cook gently until it forms a fairly thick paste. Allow to cool and store in small sealed pots.

MINT SAUCE CONCENTRATE

To every ½ lb. (*225g*) freshly picked mint leaves, allow 1 pt. (*500 ml*) apple cider vinegar *or* brown rice vinegar and 1 lb. (*450g*) sugar.

Wash and dry the leaves, chop finely and put in dry, wide necked jars. Dissolve the sugar in the vinegar stirring with a wooden spoon, allow to come to the boil and then leave to get cold. Pour over the chopped mint and seal the jars to make them airtight.

To prepare the sauce for the table: Lift out sufficient mint with a wooden spoon, together with a little of the liquid. Put into a sauce boat and add fresh apple cider vinegar or brown rice vinegar.

FRUCTOSE JAM

1 lb. (*450g*) fruit of choice   2 tspns. Gelozone
½ lb. (*225g*) fructose

Chop the fruit and stew in a little water until soft. Remove from the heat, mash and stir in the fructose. Check for sweetness and add a little more fructose, if necessary. Stir until fructose is dissolved. Mix 2 tspns. (*10 ml*) Gelozone with a little cold water. Put both mixtures into a measuring jug and top up to 1 pt. (*500 ml*) with cold water. Pour into a saucepan, bring to the boil and simmer for 2 minutes. Pot immediately into warmed jars, cover and leave until cold.

This jam does not keep well so make only a little at a time and store in the refrigerator.

LEMON CURD

Additive-free Lemon Curd is very difficult to find so here is a recipe for you to make at home.

1 oz. (*30g*) milk-free   2 large lemons
   margarine   2 eggs
½ lb. (*225g*) demerara sugar

Put the grated rind and juice from the lemons into a small basin together with the margarine and sugar. Stand the basin over a saucepan of boiling water. While this is getting hot, beat the eggs. Stir into the other ingredients and cook until thick; this takes about ½ hour. Pot and seal as for jam. Keeps very well.

ORANGE CURD

Follow the recipe and method for Lemon Curd substituting the rind and juice of 2 oranges and the juice of 1 lemon for the 2 large lemons.

Dairy Substitutes

CURD CHEESE (without rennet)

1 pt. (*500 ml*) goats' *or*
sheep's milk

1½ tblspns. lemon juice

Boil the milk and then stir in the lemon juice. Continue to boil for 1 minute until the curds separate. Leave to cool for 1 hour. Strain through muslin, and squeeze out all liquid. Tie up muslin and cover with cling-film, then press under heavy weights for several hours in the refrigerator.

Keeps 2–3 days in the refrigerator. This makes a small portion of cheese suitable for one person. For a family use 4 pts. (2¼ l.) of milk of choice and 6 tblspns. lemon juice.

For a goats' cheese with a little more body add dried goats' milk at the rate of 2 tblspns. dried goats' milk to every 1 pt. (*500 ml*) of fresh milk. Whisk the dried milk into the fresh milk before adding the lemon juice.

CURD CHEESE (with rennet)

Vegetable Rennet for cheese making is sold in Health Food Shops.

Goats':	Sheep's:
1 pt. (*500 ml*) goats' milk	1 pt. (*500 ml*) sheep's milk
2 tblspns. dried goats' milk	1 dessertspoonful rennet
1 dessertspoonful rennet	

Heat the milk to blood heat. Whisk in dried goats' milk, if using, and stir in rennet. Leave to set. Cut into cubes. Line a bowl with muslin and tip the cubes into it. Gather up muslin and suspend above a bowl. This separates the curds and whey. Leave overnight to drain. This makes a mild cheese which can be flavoured with chopped chives or other herbs of choice. It can also be used in recipes instead of cottage cheese or soft cheese.

HERBED CURD CHEESE

12 oz. (*340g*) goats' *or*	Pinch of thyme
sheep's curd cheese*	1 level tblspn. fresh parsley,
1 sm. clove garlic (optional)	finely chopped
Salt and pepper to taste	4–6 bay leaves
¼ level tspn. basil	

Sieve curd cheese into a bowl. Peel the papery coating from the garlic, trim and slice. Crush with the blade of a knife and a little salt until very fine. Add to cheese along with rest of ingredients except the bay leaves. Mix well. Press into a small bowl or turn onto a damp board and form into a round cheese shape. Press bay leaves on top or round sides and leave for several hours for the flavour to mature. Remove bay leaves before serving with a choice of crispbreads.

MOCK CREAM

1 level tblspn. arrowroot
   flour
5 tblspns. cold water

1½ oz. (*45g*) milk-free
   margarine
Sweetener to taste

Place arrowroot in a saucepan and add water, stirring all the time. Heat and stir until the mixture thickens. Beat until smooth, then put in a basin and leave until completely cold. Add margarine and beat well. Sweeten to taste and continue to beat until fluffy. Use within 2 days.

Flavourings: a few drops of orange or lemon juice, carob or raw cocoa powder, natural vanilla or a few drops of orange water or distilled rose water. Add at the final stage and beat well.

NUT CREAM

4 oz. (*110g*) cashews *or*
   blanched almonds
A little honey *or* maple
   syrup

6 tblspns. water

Grind nuts in liquidiser goblet to a fine powder. Add rest of ingredients and liquidise until smooth and creamy. Chill.

This cream has a consistency of evaporated milk and is suitable for serving with fruit salad or desserts.

NUT BUTTER

Any variety of nuts may be used. Spread the shelled nuts out on a baking tray and roast at 180°C, 350°F, Gas Mark 4 for anything up to 15 minutes, according to how roasted you like the nuts to be. Stir the nuts occasionally while they are roasting to ensure they are evenly done. Grind in liquidiser by dropping a few nuts at a time onto the rotating blades through the porthole in the lid of the liquidiser. Keep adding a little oil to make a paste and continue until contents are smooth. At the end of the process mix in a little salt to taste. The amount required is usually about ½ tspn. salt to 1 lb. (450g) nuts. Put in a jar with a wide neck and screw top. Store in the refrigerator.

NUT MILK

4 oz. (110g) cashews *or*
blanched almonds
2 pints (1.15 l) water

1–2 tblspns. (15–30 ml)
honey *or* maple syrup
(according to taste)

Grind nuts in liquidiser goblet to a fine powder. Add about ½ pint (250 ml) water and the honey or maple syrup. Liquidise until smooth and then add rest of water and liquidise again. Chill.

COCONUT MILK

3 oz. (85g) creamed coconut
¼ pt. (125 ml) hot water

Up to ¼ pt. (125 ml) cold
water

Cut the creamed coconut into pieces and put into a bowl. Pour ¼ pt. (125 ml) hot water over it and beat until coconut has completely dispersed. Leave until cold. Dilute with cold water as required. (This will depend upon what you want to use the milk for.)

Alternatively, if you want to serve it as a topping for fruit or a dessert, do not add the cold water. This will give you a thin cream similar in consistency to evaporated milk.

SUNFLOWER SEED SPREAD

8 oz. (*225g*) sunflower seeds   Salt (optional)
4 fl.oz. (*100 ml*) sunflower oil

The sunflower seeds may be lightly roasted, if desired (see Nut Butter recipe), but this is not essential. However roasting does improve the flavour.

Grind the sunflower seeds in a liquidiser until fairly fine. Gradually add the oil by pouring through the porthole in the liquidiser lid whilst the machine is running, until the oil is all incorporated and the mixture is smooth. Season to taste and store in a screw-topped jar in the refrigerator.

Other seeds which could be used are Pumpkin Seeds and Safflower Seeds.

APRICOT EGG REPLACER

12 fl.oz. (*300 ml*) water   6 oz. (*170g*) natural dried
                                    apricots

Put the water and washed apricots into a saucepan and boil until the apricots are soft. Leave to cool, then blend in a liquidiser. Store in the refrigerator. 2 tblspns. = 1 egg.

DATE EGG REPLACER

12 fl.oz. (*300 ml*) water   6 oz. (*170g*) dates, pitted

Put the water and dates into a saucepan and boil until the dates are soft. Leave to cool, then blend in a liquidiser. Store in the refrigerator. 2 tblspns. = 1 egg.

The above two egg replacers are suitable for binding and bulking in waffles, pancakes, drop scones and heavier cakes. They are not suitable where aeration is required.

Drinks

LEMONADE

2 large *or* 3 small lemons
2 lb. (*900g*) sugar *or* 1¼ lb.
   (*560g*) fructose

½ oz. (*15g*) citric acid *or*
¼ oz. (*8g*) malic acid
1½ pt. (*750 ml*) boiling water

Wash fruit thoroughly. Squeeze out juice and put into a mixing bowl. Remove pith and put peel through mincer. Add the sugar or fructose and mix together. Pour on boiling water, stir to dissolve sugar and leave overnight (covered). Next day add the acid of choice, a little at a time, checking between each addition until the flavour is right. Put through a strainer or muslin bag and bottle. Keep in refrigerator and dilute to taste as requred.

BLACKBERRY SYRUP

Stew the blackberries with ¼ pt. (*125 ml*) water to every 3 lb. (*1 kg 350g*) fruit, until all the juice is drawn. Strain, and for every 1 pt. (*500 ml*) juice add 6 oz. (*170g*) sugar. Boil for 15 minutes and bottle for use when cold. Serve diluted to taste with hot or cold water.

As this syrup contains no preservatives, store the bottles in the refrigerator. It makes a pleasant drink for cold winter evenings when diluted with hot water.

TRADITIONAL LEMON BARLEY WATER

3 oz. (*85g*) pearl barley
1 medium-sized lemon

1–1½ oz. (*30–45g*) sugar *or*
½–¾ oz. (*15–25g*) fructose

Put the pearl barley into a saucepan and cover with cold water. Bring to boil and boil for 5 minutes. Drain. Add 2 pts. (*1 l*) cold water and bring back to boil. Cover and simmer for 30 minutes. Wash and thinly peel the lemon (yellow only). Add to saucepan and continue to simmer for a further 30 minutes. Squeeze out juice from lemon and strain. Put aside. Strain liquid in saucepan into a bowl or jug and add sweetener to taste. When cold stir in lemon juice.

Bottle and store in the refrigerator.
Keeps up to 1 week.

BLACKCURRANT BARLEY WATER

Barley Water is traditionally made with pearl barley but is equally good and much quicker to make using barley flakes.

8 oz. (*225g*) blackcurrants　　　2 oz. (*55g*) barley flakes
3 pts. (*1.7 l*) water　　　　　　　Sugar *or* other sweetener to
　　　　　　　　　　　　　　　　taste

Stew the blackcurrants in the water until the juice is extracted. Add the barley flakes and continue to cook until the mixture thickens. Line a bowl with muslin and strain out all the juice. Serve hot or cold. Diluted if you prefer, and sweeten to taste.

This drink is good for coughs and colds, so keep some blackcurrants in the freezer in readiness for the winter.

GINGER BEER

1 lb. (*450g*) demerara sugar　　　½ oz. (*15g*) cream of tartar
1 lemon, sliced　　　　　　　　　½ oz. (*15g*) dried yeast
2 oz. (*55g*) root ginger　　　　　1 gallon (*4½ l*) boiling water

Put sugar, sliced lemon, ginger and cream of tartar into a large container and pour the boiling water over them. Allow to cool to blood heat, then add the yeast and leave for 24 hours in a warm place. Strain through muslin and pour into strong bottles with a screw top. Store for 3–4 days when the Ginger Beer will be ready to drink.

Sweets

HONEYCOMB

8 oz. (*225g*) sugar
Small pinch of cream of
    tartar
4 tblspns. cold water

1 tblspn. golden syrup
¼ tspn. bicarbonate of soda
A little warm water

Put the sugar, cream of tartar, syrup and cold water into a
strong pan. Stir over low heat until sugar has dissolved. Boil
without stirring to 310°F (on a sugar thermometer). Remove
from heat. Mix the bicarbonate of soda with a little warm
water and add to the boiling hot toffee. (It will froth up in the
pan). Stir gently and pour into a greased or oiled tin.

TURKISH DELIGHT

1 lb. (*450g*) granulated sugar
¼ level tspn. cream of tartar
3½ oz. (*100g*) cornflour
7½ oz. (*215g*) icing sugar

2 oz. (*55g*) clear honey
2 tspns. distilled rose water
Natural red colouring
(optional)

Lightly grease or oil a shallow 7" square tin. Place granulated sugar and ¼ pt. (*125 ml*) water in a heavy-based saucepan. Stir over a moderate heat until sugar has dissolved. Bring to boil and boil quickly, without stirring, until 'soft-ball' stage is reached (240°F on a sugar thermometer, or until a little, when dropped in a saucer of cold water, will just form a soft ball). Remove from heat, stir in cream of tartar and then leave on one side. While syrup is cooling mix 3 oz. (*85g*) cornflour and 7 oz. (*200g*) icing sugar in a large saucepan with a little cold water, taken from a measured 1 pt. (*500 ml*). Add remaining water. Bring to the boil, stirring all the time and cook for 2 minutes. Reduce heat and gradually pour the cooled syrup into the cornflour mixture, beating well with a wooden spoon. Bring to the boil and boil for 20–30 minutes over a low heat, stirring continuously, when mixture should be very pale straw in colour and transparent.

Add honey and rosewater, mix thoroughly. Pour half the mixture into prepared tin. Put a tablespoonful (*15 ml*) of the remainder into a cup, add a little natural red food colouring and mix well. Add the coloured mixture to the remainder left in the pan and mix well. Pour over the mixture already in the tin. Leave until quite cold. Dip a sharp knife into icing sugar and cut Turkish Delight into 1" bars. Mix ½ oz. (*15g*) cornflour with ½ oz. (*15g*) icing sugar and roll bars in mixture to coat evenly. Leave for 3–4 hours, then cut into 1" squares and coat again in mixture. Leave overnight. Pack.

Makes 49 pieces.

COCONUT ICE

1 lb. (*450g*) granulated sugar
¼ pt. (*125 ml*) goats' *or*
 sheep's milk

5 oz. (*140g*) desiccated
 coconut (preservative-
 free)
Natural red colouring
 (optional)

Brush a 7" square tin with oil or melted milk-free margarine.

Place sugar and milk in a heavy-based saucepan. Stir over a low heat until sugar has dissolved. Bring to boil and boil quickly, without stirring, for about 10 minutes, until 'soft-ball' stage is reached (240°F on a sugar thermometer, or until a little, when dropped in a saucer of cold water, just forms a soft ball.) Remove saucepan from heat; add coconut and stir until mixture begins to thicken. Pour half the mixture into prepared tin. Put a tablespoonful (*15 ml*) of the remainder into a cup, add a little natural red food colouring and mix well. Add the coloured mixture to the remainder left in the pan and mix well. Pour coloured mixture over that already in the tin. Leave until almost set; mark into 10 bars. When cold, turn out of tin and cut into bars.

Makes 10 bars.

CHOCOLATE OR CAROB FUDGE

8 oz. (*225g*) date palm sugar
1 oz. (*30g*) milk-free
 margarine

2½ level tblspns. raw cocoa
 powder *or* carob powder

Put date palm sugar into a saucepan and dissolve over very low heat. Do not allow it to boil. Add margarine and stir until it melts, then add sieved cocoa or carob and beat well. Quickly pour into well-oiled small shallow tin and leave until completely cold. Cut into 1" cubes.

PEPPERMINT FUDGE

8 oz. (*225g*) date palm sugar   3 drops oil of peppermint
1 level tblspn. soya flour   B.P.

Put date palm sugar into a saucepan and dissolve over very low heat. Do not allow it to boil. Add sieved soya flour and mix. Finally, add peppermint oil and beat well. Quickly pour into a well-oiled small shallow tin and leave until completely cold. Cut into 1" cubes.

NUT BRITTLE

4 oz. (*110g*) icing sugar   1 tspn. lemon juice
2–4 oz. (*55–110g*) nuts of
   choice

Blanch, roast and chop the nuts. Sieve sugar if lumpy, and put with lemon juice into a pan over gentle heat. Heat until golden brown. DO NOT BEAT but stir very gently with a wooden spoon until evenly browned. Stir in finely chopped nuts. Pour onto a greased or oiled tin. Mark whilst warm into squares. Break when cold and store in an airtight jar.

HONEY AND TREACLE TOFFEE

4 tblspns. water
4 oz. (*110g*) milk-free
    margarine
1 lb. 2 oz. (*510g*) muscovado
    sugar

2 tblspns. clear honey
1 tblspn. black treacle

Put all the ingredients in a pan. Heat slowly, stirring until sugar dissolves and margarine melts. Bring to the boil, then cover pan and boil gently for 2 minutes. Uncover and continue to boil, stirring occasionally, for 10–15 minutes (or until a little of the mixture, dropped into a cup of cold water, separates into hard and brittle threads). Pour into greased 6″ square tin and leave until hard, then break with a small hammer. Store in a screw-topped jar.

TREACLE BITES

4½ oz. (*125g*) rye, barley,
    millet *or* buckwheat
    flakes
1 oz. (*30g*) rye, barley, millet
    or buckwheat flour
½ tspn. wheat-free baking
    powder
¼ tspn. salt

1 oz. (*30g*) milk-free
    margarine
1 oz. (*30g*) demerara sugar
1 egg, beaten
Pinch of natural vanilla
3 tblspns. black treacle
A little grated lemon rind
    (optional)

Sieve flour, baking powder and salt together. Melt milk-free margarine in a saucepan together with the black treacle. Mix all ingredients well. Drop from a teaspoon in rounds 1½″ apart onto a greased baking sheet. Bake at 190°C, 375°F, Gas Mark 5 for 10–15 minutes.

Makes 12

FRUIT AND NUT BARS

3 oz. (*85g*) natural raisins *or* dates

1½ oz. (*45g*) figs *or* desiccated coconut (preservative-free)

1½ oz. (*45g*) nuts

1 eating apple *or* banana

1 tblspn. fruit juice

Approx. 2 oz. (*55g*) soya flour *or* powdered goats' milk

Put first four ingredients through a mincer into a bowl. Add juice and mix thoroughly. Add soya flour or powdered goats' milk and mix to a firm dry paste. Turn onto a piece of rice paper and press down firmly to ½" thickness or less. Chill. Cut into bars.

NUT BUTTER FUDGE

6 level tblspns. Nut Butter*

6 level tblspns. set honey

4 oz. (*110g*) powdered goats' *or* soya milk

Mix together the nut butter and honey and then stir in the powdered milk. Mix well and turn onto oiled greaseproof paper. Flatten into a ½" thick bar. Cut into cubes and chill.

TRUFFLES

6 level tblspns. honey
6 level tblspns. Nut Butter*
¾ oz. (*20g*) soya flour *or*
   powdered goats' milk
1 oz. (*30g*) millet flakes
1 oz. (*30g*) buckwheat flakes

1½ oz. (*45g*) nuts, roasted
   and finely chopped
3 level tblspns. raw cocoa
   powder *or* carob powder
1 tspn. lemon rind, grated
2 tspns. rum (optional)

Mix all ingredients together. Form into small balls, and roll them in either cocoa, carob, ground nuts or desiccated coconut. Put into paper sweet cases.

NOUGAT CANDIES

3½ oz. (*100g*) Bournville
   Plain chocolate *or* Plamil
   Carob Bar
1 tblspn. black treacle
1 tblspn. honey

2 oz. (*55g*) porridge oats,
   buckwheat *or* millet
   flakes
2 oz. (*55g*) natural raisins,
   chopped

Melt the chocolate or carob with the treacle and honey in a bowl over a saucepan of hot water. Mix in the flakes and raisins. Spoon into sweet cases.
Makes 20.

APPENDIX I

PLANT FOOD FAMILIES

LATIN	ENGLISH	
Aceraceae	Acer	Maple
Actinidiaceae	Kiwi	Kiwi fruit (Chinese gooseberry)
Amaranthaceae	Amaranth	Amaranth
Anacardiaceae	Cashew	Pistachio, mango, cashew
Ananas	Pineapple	Pineapple
Anonaceae	Sop	Sour sop, sweet sop, cherimoya
Aquifoliaceae	Holly	Mate tea
Araceae	Arum	Taro, eddo, dasheen, tannia, ceriman
Boraginaceae	Borage	Comfrey, borage
Cannabiaceae	Hemp	Hop
Capparidaceae	Caper	Caper
Caprifoliaceae	Honeysuckle	Elderberry
Caricaceae	Papaya	Pawpaw, papaya
Chenopodiaceae	Goosefoot	Spinach, sugarbeet, beetroot, swiss chard, orache, Good King Henry
Compositae	Daisy	Chicory, dandelion, tarragon, lettuce, alecost, sunflower, cardoon, wormwood, chamomile, Jerusalem artichoke, endive, globe artichoke, sesame, safflower, chinese leaves, salsify, scorzonera, feverfew, tansy, radichio rosso, pot marigold
Convolvulaceae	Bindweed	Sweet potato
Corylaceae	Birch	Filberts, hazelnuts, cobnuts
Cruciferae	Wallflower	Mustard, radish, turnip, horseradish, cabbage, watercress, broccoli, calabrese, cress, cauliflower, kale, kohlrabi, brussel sprouts, swede (rutabaga), seakale, rocket, rapeseed, chinese greens (pak-choi, pe-tsai, wong bok and shungiku)
Cucurbitaceae	Gourd	Cucumber, pumpkin, melon, courgette, watermelon, squash, gherkin, marrow, chayote, gourd, zucchini
Cupressaceae	Cypress	Juniper berries
Cyperaceae	Sedge	Chinese water chestnut

Dioscorea	Yam	Yam, chinese yam (chinese potato)
Diospyros	Ebony	Persimmon
Ericaceae	Erica	Blueberry, arbutus (strawberry tree), cranberry, bilberry, cowberry, whortleberry
Euphorbiaceae	Spurge	Tapioca (manioc, cassava)
Fagaceae	Beech	Sweet chestnut
Fungi		Mushroom, yeast, truffle
Graminae	Grass	Wheat, corn (maize, sweet corn), rice, oats, barley, rye, cane, millet, bamboo, sorghum, wild rice
Grossulariaceae	Gooseberry	Gooseberry, blackcurrant, red currant, white currant
Iridaceae	Iris	Saffron
Juglans	Walnut	Butternut, hickory nut, walnut, pecan
Labiatae	Mint	Peppermint, spearmint, thyme, marjoram, basil, oregano, sweet basil, summer savory, winter savory, sage, rosemary, lemon balm, bergamot, hyssop
Lauraceae	Laurel	Avocado, cinnamon, bay leaf
Leguminosae or Papilionaceae	Legume or Pea	Pea, all varieties of dried beans, soya, lima beans, lentils, peanuts, groundnuts, liquorice, carob, gram, mung beans, alfalfa, chick pea, broad bean, French bean, runner bean, fenugreek, tamarind, Morton Bay chestnut
Liliaceae	Lily	Asparagus *Sub. species Allium* onion, garlic, chives, leeks, spring onions, kurrat, shallots, scallion
Linaceae	Flax	Flax (linseed)
Malvaceae	Mallow	Okra pods, cotton seed, hibiscus flowers
Moraceae	Mulberry	Fig, mulberry, breadfruit, jackfruit
Musaceae	Banana	Banana, arrowroot, plantain
Myristica	Nutmeg	Nutmeg, mace
Myrtaceae	Myrtle	Allspice, pimento, cloves, guava
Nymphaeaceae	Water Lily	Lotus
Oleaceae	Olive	Olive
Onagraceae	Willow-herb	Water chestnut, singhara nut
Orchidaceae	Orchid	Vanilla
Palmae	Palm	Coconut, date, sago, palm oil, date palm sugar
Papaveraceae	Poppy	Poppy seed
Passiflora	Passionflower	Passion fruit, giant granadilla
Pinaceae	Pine	Pine nuts
Piperaceae	Peppercorns	Black and white peppercorns

Polygonaceae	Knotweed	Buckwheat, rhubarb, sorrel
Proteacea	Macadamia	Macadamia or Queensland nut
Punicaceae	Pomegranate	Pomegranate
Rosaceae	Rose	Apple, pear, quince, japonica quince, medlar, loquat, crab-apple, rowan, azarole, rosehip, strawberry, salad burnet, service tree (sorbitol)
		Sub, genus Prunus plum, peach, cherry, apricot, almond, nectarine, sloe, damson, bullace, greengage
		Sub. genus Rubus raspberry, cloudberry, loganberry, blackberry, wineberry, dewberry, boysenberry
Rubiaceae	Madder	Coffee
Rutaceae	Citrus	Lemon, grapefruit, tangerine, orange, satsuma, lime, citron, kumquat, ugli fruit, clementine
Sapindaceae	Lychee	Rambutan, lychee
Solanaceae	Potato	Tomato, potato, eggplant (aubergine), chilli, sweet pepper (capsicum), cayenne, ground cherries, tomatillo (jamberry), cape gooseberry, huckleberry, paprika
Subcaya	Brazil Nut	Brazil nut
Theaceae	Camellia	Tea
Theobroma	Cocoa	Cocoa
Umbelliferae	Hemlock	Carrot, parsnip, celery, anise, parsley, caraway, celeriac, dill, coriander, fennel, cumin, chervil, lovage, celery seed, angelica, samphire, sweet cicely
Urticaceae	Nettle	Nettle
Vitaceae	Vine	Grape, raisin, sultana, currant, cream of tartar
Zingiberaceae	Ginger	Ginger, turmeric, curcumin

APPENDIX II

VITAMIN AND MINERAL SOURCES

This section is a relatively comprehensive list of vitamins and minerals, and of foods containing them. The purpose is that those on special diets, whether for medical, moral or other reasons, can use the list to ensure that they are getting reasonable amounts of the necessary vitamins and minerals from the selection of foods they eat. (Supplements may be necessary in some cases.)

As a guide in qualitative terms, the foods indicated in bold capital letters are extremely good sources, those in capitals are useful sources, while those in lower case type contain smaller but still reasonable amounts. However, it should be noted that in some categories this information is not available and all the foods appear in lower case letters.

If you are on a diet where many foods are excluded, we suggest that you go through the lists, crossing out the foods you cannot have; you will then be left with a choice of acceptable alternatives. Both animal and vegetable sources of nutrients are included for the sake of completeness.

VITAMIN A (RETINOL)

Needed for skin and eyes, respiration, digestion, glands and bowel function. Deficiency leads to accident proneness, hay fever, allergy, slowness, poor bone growth, breathing disorders, sore mouth and gums, and general susceptibility to disease.

Found in: ALFALFA, apricots (fresh), APRICOTS (DRIED), ASPARAGUS, asparagus bean, avocado pear, black-eyed pea, BROAD BEAN, BROCCOLI, BRUSSEL SPROUTS, BUTTER, cabbage, capsicum (sweet peppers), CARROTS, cashews, cauliflower, cheese, chick peas, **COD LIVER OIL**, comfrey, corn oil, currants, dandelion, dates, EELS, EGGS, ENDIVE, fenugreek sprouts, figs (fresh), FRENCH BEANS, **HALIBUT LIVER OIL**, herrings, kelp, kidneys, leeks, lentils, lettuce, lima beans, maize (corn), mango, melon (canteloupe), MILK (COWS', GOATS', SHEEP'S), mung beans, mustard and cress, nectarines, okra pods, olive oil, LIVER, PAPAYA, paprika, PARSLEY, pawpaw, PEACHES (DRIED), peas (fresh and dried), pecans, pineapple, pistachio nuts, PRUNES, pumpkin seeds, RUNNER BEANS, sardines, soya beans, SPINACH, SPRING GREENS, sunflower seeds, sweet chestnuts, sweet corn, **SWEET POTATO**, tomato, TOMATO **PURÉE, TURNIP TOPS**, walnuts, WATERCRESS, WHEATGERM, yoghurt (live).

VITAMIN B1 (THIAMINE)

Necessary for proper function of respiratory system, heart, nervous system and muscles. Deficiency leads to weaknesses in these systems and impaired growth in children.

Found in: Aduki beans, ADUKI BEAN SPROUTS, ALFALFA, ALMONDS, alphatoco sprouts, apricots (dried), asparagus, asparagus bean, asparagus pea, avocado pear, bacon, barley, beef, beer, bladderwrack, black-eyed pea, bran (wheat), **BRAZIL NUTS**, BREWERS' YEAST, broad bean, broccoli, brown rice, BUCKWHEAT, cabbage, carrot, cashews, CAULIFLOWER, celeriac, celery, CHEESE, CHICK PEAS, cocoa, coconut, COD, COD'S ROE, comfrey, CRAB, currants, dates, damsons, DUCK, dulse, EGGS, ENDIVE, fenugreek, figs, **GROUSE**, haddock, HAZELNUTS, HEART, herring's roe, HONEY, horseradish, JERUSALEM ARTICHOKE, KELP, KIDNEYS, lamb, leeks, LENTILS, lentil sprouts, LETTUCE, lima beans, liver, lobster, maize (corn), **MARMITE**, milk (cows', goats', sheep's), millet, MOLASSES, mung bean sprouts, MUSHROOMS, **OAT BRAN & OAT GERM**, oatmeal, OKRA PODS, oranges, oysters, PARSLEY, PARSNIPS, PEANUTS, PEAS (FRESH & DRIED), pecans, pheasant, pineapple, PLAICE, PORK, POTATOES, prunes, RABBIT, raisins, **RICE GERM**, runner beans, rye, sardines, scampi, seakale, **SESAME SEEDS**, sorghum, soya beans, spring greens, sultanas, SUNFLOWER SEEDS, swedes, sweet chestnuts, SWEET CORN, sweet potatoes, tangerines, tomatoes, TOMATO PURÉE, tuna, TURKEY, turnip tops, VENI-

SON, WALNUTS, WATERCRESS, WHEATGERM, wholemeal flour, WILD RICE, yams, yeast (fresh), **YEAST (DRIED), YEAST EXTRACT**, yoghurt (live).

VITAMIN B2 (RIBOFLAVIN)

Essential for building and maintaining body tissues. Signs of deficiency are a sore tongue and sores at the corners of the mouth; it is also thought that the eyes can become oversensitive to light.

Found in: Aduki beans, ADUKI BEAN SPROUTS, almonds, alphatoco sprouts, apricots (dried), asparagus, asparagus bean, avocado pear, BACON, barley, beef, beer, black-eyed pea, bran (wheat), brazil nuts, BREWER'S YEAST, broad bean, BROCCOLI, brown rice, brussel sprouts, BUCK-WHEAT, cashews, cauliflower, cheese, CHICKEN, chick pea, coconut, cod, COD'S ROE, comfrey, CRAB, dates, DUCK, eggs, ENDIVE, **GROUSE**, haddock, HERRING, herring's roe, KELP, KIDNEYS, LAMB, LENTILS, LENTIL SPROUTS, lettuce, lima beans, liver, MACKEREL, maize (corn), **MARMITE**, mayonnaise, MILK (COWS', GOATS', SHEEP'S), millet, molasses, mung beans, MUNG BEAN SPROUTS, MUSHROOMS, OAT BRAN & OAT GERM, OATMEAL, OKRA PODS, OYSTERS, PARSLEY, parsnip, passion fruit, peaches (dried), peanuts, peas (fresh and dried), pecans, PHEASANT, plaice, pork, potatoes, PRUNES, pumpkin seeds, runner beans, rye, salmon, sardines, SESAME SEEDS, sorghum, soya beans, spinach, SPRING GREENS, sunflower seeds, sweet chestnuts, tuna, TURKEY, walnuts, watercress, WHEATGERM, wholemeal flour, **WILD RICE**, YEAST EXTRACT, yeast (fresh), YEAST (DRIED), yoghurt (live).

VITAMIN B3 (NIACIN, NICOTINIC ACID, NICOTINAMIDE)

Necessary for converting food into energy; needed for the nervous system, appetite and healthy skin. Signs of deficiency are skin lesions, rashes, mouth ulcers and diarrhoea.

Found in: Aduki beans, aduki bean sprouts, alfalfa sprouts, ALMONDS, alphatoco sprouts, APRICOTS (DRIED), asparagus bean, asparagus pea, BACON, BARLEY, BEEF, beer, black-eyed pea, **BRAN (WHEAT)**, BRAZIL NUTS, BREWER'S YEAST, BROAD BEANS, broccoli, BROWN RICE, BUCKWHEAT, cashews, celeriac, cheese, CHICKEN, chicory, COCOA, coconut, COD, COD'S ROE, COMFREY, CRAB, currants, DATES, DUCK, **EGGS**, figs, **GROUSE**, HADDOCK, **HAZELNUTS**, HERRING, HONEY, KELP, KIDNEYS, LAMB, leeks, lentils, lentil sprouts, lima beans, **LIVER**, MACKEREL, MAIZE (CORN), **MARMITE**, milk (cows', goats', sheep's), MILLET, mung beans, MUNG BEAN SPROUTS, MUSHROOMS, oatmeal, okra pods, papaya, parsley, parsnips, PEACHES (DRIED), **PEANUTS**, peas (fresh and dried), pecans, PHEASANT, PIGEON, PLAICE, PORK, potatoes, pumpkin seeds, RABBIT, raisins, runner beans, rye, SALMON, sardines, SESAME SEEDS, SHRIMPS, SORGHUM, SOYA BEANS, sultanas, SUNFLOWER SEEDS, sweet chestnuts, TOMATO PURÉE, **TUNA**, TURKEY, VENISON, walnuts, whelks, WHEATGERM, WHOLEMEAL FLOUR, WILD RICE, **YEAST EXTRACT**, YEAST (FRESH), YEAST (DRIED), yoghurt (live).

VITAMIN B5 (PANTOTHENIC ACID)

Essential for tissue growth, healthy skin and hair. Signs of deficiency are fatigue and muscle cramps.

Found in: Aduki sprouts, alfalfa sprouts, alphatoco sprouts, avocado pear, barley, BRAN (WHEAT), BREWER'S YEAST, BROAD BEANS, brown rice, buckwheat, cheese, cod, COD'S ROE, COMFREY, dates, eggs, haddock, herring, HONEY, KELP, KIDNEYS, lamb, lentil sprouts, LIVER, lobster, mackerel, milk (cows', goats', sheep's), molasses, mung bean sprouts, MUSHROOMS, oatmeal, peanuts, plaice, raisins, rye, SALMON, sardines, soya beans, tuna, WHEATGERM, wholemeal flour, YEAST EXTRACT, YEAST (FRESH), **YEAST (DRIED)**.

VITAMIN B6 (PYRIDOXINE)

Important for healthy teeth and gums, the health of blood vessels, red blood cells and the nervous system. Necessary for converting foods into energy. Deficiency can cause depression, irritability, skin problems, diarrhoea and anaemia.

Found in: Aduki sprouts, alfalfa sprouts, ALMONDS, alphatoco sprouts, APRICOTS (DRIED), apricots (fresh), avocado pear, bacon, banana, barley, beef, BEER, beetroot, bilberries, blackcurrants, BRAN (WHEAT), BRAZIL NUTS, BREWER'S YEAST, broccoli, brown rice, BRUSSEL SPROUTS, buckwheat, cabbage, CAPSICUM (SWEET PEPPER), carrots, cauliflower, celeriac, celery, cheese, cherries, CHICKEN, chicory, cocoa, COD, COD'S ROE, comfrey, CRAB, cucumber, dates, damsons, DUCK, **EGGS**, figs, grapes, greengages, HADDOCK, HAZELNUTS, HERRING, HONEY, HORSERADISH, **KIDNEYS**, LAMB, LEEKS, lemons, lentils, lentil sprouts, LETTUCE, **LIVER,** loganberries, MACKEREL, **MARMITE**, MARROW, mayonnaise, melons, milk (cows', goats', sheep's), MOLASSES, mulberries, MUNG BEAN SPROUTS, oat bran and oat germ, oatmeal, OKRA PODS, ONIONS, oranges, oysters, PARSNIPS, PEACHES (DRIED), PEANUTS, PEAS (FRESH AND DRIED), pineapple, PLAICE, PLANTAIN, PORK, port, potatoes, PRUNES, pumpkin, pumpkin seeds, RABBIT, radishes, raisins, raspberries, rye, SALMON, SARDINES, SHRIMPS, soya beans, SPINACH, SPRING ONIONS, STOUT, strawberries, sultanas, SUNFLOWER SEEDS, SWEDE, sweet chestnuts, sweet corn, SWEET POTATO, tangerines, tomato, TOMATO PURÉE, TUNA, TURKEY, TURNIP TOPS, veal, **WALNUTS**, watercress, WHEATGERM, wholemeal flour, WINES, **YEAST (FRESH), YEAST (DRIED).**

VITAMIN B12 (CYANOCOBALAMIN)

Essential for healthy blood function; contributes to a healthy nervous system and is important for growth in children. Deficiency can result in pernicious anaemia.

Found in: Aduki bean sprouts, ALE, alfalfa sprouts, alpha-toco sprouts, avocado pear, barley, beef, BEER, bladderwrack, BREWER'S YEAST, buckwheat, cheese, COD, COD'S ROE, COMFREY, EGGS, HADDOCK, HERRING, kelp, **KIDNEYS**, lamb, lentil sprouts, lettuce, **LIVER**, LOBSTER, MACKEREL, MARMITE, marrow, milk (cows', goats', sheep's), molasses, mung bean sprouts, MUSHROOMS, **OKRA PODS**, ONIONS, **OYSTERS**, parsnips, PLAICE, PORK, RABBIT, raisins, SALMON, SARDINES, SHRIMPS, **SPRING ONIONS**, STOUT, turkey, VEAL, wheatgerm.

VITAMIN C (ASCORBIC ACID)

Important for building up the immune system, for the health of connective tissues and muscles, glandular tissues and sex organs, and for the proper absorption of protein and calcium. Deficiency leads to the inability to resist infections, eye troubles, bleeding gums and wounds that do not heal easily. Large doses can cut short a threatening cold and are claimed to be very beneficial in the treatment of many infections and diseases including cancer.

Found in: Aduki sprouts, alfalfa sprouts, alphatoco sprouts, apples (cooking), apricots (dried), ASPARAGUS, asparagus bean, avocado pear, banana, beetroot, BEET TOPS, BILBER-RIES, BLACKBERRIES, **BLACKCURRANTS**, black-eyed pea, BROAD BEAN, BROCCOLI, BRUSSEL SPROUTS, CABB-AGE, canteloupe melon, CAPSICUM (SWEET PEPPER), carrot, CAULIFLOWER, celeriac, CELERY, chervil, chick pea, chilli pepper, comfrey, cucumber, dandelion, ELDERBER-RIES, ENDIVE, fenugreek sprouts, French beans, garlic, GRAPEFRUIT, GOOSEBERRIES, GUAVA, HONEY, hon-eydew melon, HORSERADISH, kale, kelp, KIDNEY, KIWI FRUIT, KOHLRABI, LEEKS, LEMON, lentil sprouts, LET-TUCE, LIVER, loganberries, LYCHEES, MANGO, mulber-ries, mung bean sprouts, MUSTARD AND CRESS, ORANGE, onion, PAPAYA, paprika, **PARSLEY**, PARSNIP, peas, pineapple, plantain, pot marigold, POTATO, pumpkin seeds, radish, raspberries, redcurrants, rooibosch tea, rose-hips, runner beans, SEAKALE, SPINACH, SPRING GREENS,

SPRING ONIONS, strawberries, SWEDE, sweet corn, SWEET POTATO, TOMATO, turnips, **TURNIP TOPS, WATERCRESS**, yoghurt (live).

VITAMIN D (CALCIFEROL)

Vital for balance of calcium and phosphorus, for heart efficiency, muscle tone and nervous stability. Deficiency leads to bone and teeth troubles and heart and muscle weakness.

Found in: Alfalfa sprouts, BUTTER, CHEESE, **COD LIVER OIL**, corn oil, EGGS, funugreek sprouts, FISH (most), **HALIBUT LIVER OIL**, kelp, MILK (COWS', GOATS', SHEEP'S), olive oil, parsley, safflower oil, sunflower oil, watercress, wheatgerm.

VITAMIN E (TOCOPHEROL)

Essential for heart, liver and glandular efficiency. Deficiency leads to lack of muscle tone and inhibits supply of oxygen to the tissues.

Found in: ALFALFA SPROUTS, **ALMONDS**, alphatoco sprouts, ASPARAGUS, avocado pear, blackberries, BLADDERWRACK, BRAZIL NUTS, BROWN RICE, butter, carrots, CHEESE, cod liver oil, COD'S ROE, comfrey, corn oil, DANDELION LEAVES, dulse, EGG YOLK, **HAZELNUTS**, KELP, laverbread, LETTUCE, LINSEED, **LIVER**, lobster, mayonnaise, **OAT BRAN & OAT GERM**, olive oil, parsley, PEANUTS, SESAME SEEDS, spinach, SUNFLOWER SEEDS, sweet potatoes, tomato purée, WATERCRESS, WHEATGERM, wholemeal flour, yoghurt (live).

VITAMIN H (BIOTIN)

Involved in protein synthesis and essential for healthy mucous membranes, skin, red blood cells and cardiovascular system. Deficiency can cause dermatitis and muscle pains.

Found in: BRAN (WHEAT), BREWER'S YEAST, cheese, COD'S ROE, EGGS, HONEY, HERRINGS, **KIDNEY, LIVER**, milk (cows', goats', sheep's), molasses, OATMEAL, OYSTERS, raisins, wholemeal flour, YEAST (FRESH), **YEAST (DRIED).**

VITAMIN K (PHYTOMENADIONE, PHYLLOQUINONE)

Needed by the blood to facilitate clotting ability.

Found in: ALFALFA SPROUTS, CHESTNUTS, egg yolks, olive oil, peanuts, SOYA BEANS.

VITAMIN M [OR Bc] (FOLIC ACID)

Works in conjunction with Vitamin B12 in blood formation and is essential for a healthy digestive system. Deficiency can cause anaemia, particularly in pregnant women.

Found in: ADUKI BEAN SPROUTS, ALFALFA SPROUTS, ALMONDS, ALPHATOCO SPROUTS, asparagus, avocado pear, BEETROOT, BRAN (WHEAT), BREWER'S YEAST, BROCCOLI, BRUSSEL SPROUTS, buckwheat, cabbage, CALABRESE, cauliflower, celery, CHEESE, CHICORY, cucumber, eggs, ENDIVE, HAZELNUTS, haricot beans, HONEY, kale, kidney, **LIVER, MARMITE**, milk (cows', goats', sheep's), MUNG BEAN SPROUTS, mustard, oatmeal, OKRA PODS, parsley, PEANUTS, rye, spinach, SPRING GREENS, tangerines, TOMATO PURÉE, turnip tops, WALNUTS, watercress, WHEATGERM, **WHITE FISH**, wholemeal flour, **YEAST (FRESH), YEAST (DRIED).**

VITAMIN P (BIOFLAVANOIDS)

Works in conjunction with Vitamin C.

Found in: Buckwheat, citrus fruits, grapes, paprika, plums, rosehips.

SULPHUR

Is good for the brain and nervous system. An adequate supply prevents premature senility. Deficiency leads to bronchial, digestive, optical and skin problems.

Found in: **ALL FISH, MEAT, POULTRY AND GAME,** ALMONDS, APRICOTS (DRIED), BARLEY, black treacle, bran (wheat), **BRAZIL NUTS,** brown rice, brussel sprouts, butter beans, cabbage (raw), **CHEDDAR CHEESE,** chick peas, coconut (desiccated), curry powder, EGGS, dates, figs, GINGER, haricot beans, hazelnuts, **HORSERADISH,** LENTIL SPROUTS, **MILK POWDER,** molasses, mung beans, MUNG BEAN SPROUTS, mushrooms, **MUSTARD,** MUSTARD AND CRESS, OATMEAL, onions, **PARMESAN CHEESE, PEACHES (DRIED), PEANUTS,** peas, pepper, roast potatoes, seakale, spinach, spring onions, **STILTON CHEESE,** WALNUTS, WATERCRESS.

ZINC

Needed for muscular control and good digestion. Controls the ability to taste and is important for diabetics.

Found in: All meat and poultry, almonds, arrowroot, **BRAN (WHEAT),** brazil nuts, brown rice, butter beans, cheese, COCOA, CRAB, eggs, GINGER, haricot beans, hazelnuts, lentils, lentil sprouts, lobster, Marmite, milk powder, MUSTARD, oat bran & oat germ, oatmeal, **OYSTERS,** peanuts, peas (dried), pepper, rye, sardines, SHRIMPS, sweet corn, tomato purée, walnuts, WHELKS, wholemeal flour, WINKLES, YEAST (DRIED), yeast (fresh).

COPPER

Helps with formation of red blood cells in conjunction with iron, and is also needed for bone growth. Deficiency leads to diarrhoea (particularly in babies), and changes in hair texture and colour.

Found in: Almonds, apricots (dried), arrowroot, asparagus, avocado pear, black treacle, BRAN (WHEAT), BRAZIL NUTS, broad beans, **CALF LIVER**, chestnuts, chick peas, COCOA, coconut, **CRAB**, CURRY POWDER, dates, duck, egg yolk, figs, ginger, goose, hazelnuts, **LAMB'S LIVER**, lemons, lentil sprouts, lobster, Marmite, milk powder, molasses, mung bean sprouts, mushrooms, mustard, oatmeal, offal, olives, OX LIVER, **OYSTERS**, parsley, peaches (dried), peanuts, peas, PEPPER, **PIG'S LIVER**, raisins, raspberries, rye, salmon, shrimps, spinach, sultanas, tomato purée, walnuts, WHEATGERM, **WHELKS**, wholemeal flour, WINKLES, **YEAST (DRIED)**, yeast (fresh).

CALCIUM

As well as being needed for teeth and bones, calcium is also used by the body to assist in blood clotting and heart efficiency. It is also important for the vitality of cells, and during convalescence. Deficiency leads to rickets, rheumatic pain and brittle bones during old age.

Found in: ADUKI BEANS, ALFALFA, almonds, ASPARAGUS PEA/BEAN, barley, black-eyed pea, BLACK TREACLE, bran (wheat), brazil nuts, buckwheat, CAROB, carrageen, chamomile flowers, CHEESE, chives, cider vinegar, cocoa, comfrey, currants, CURRY POWDER, dandelion root, egg yolk, figs, flax seeds, garlic, honey, horseradish, lemon, lime, milk (cows', goats', sheep's), **MILK POWDER**, millet, MOLASSES, mung bean sprouts, mustard, nettles, oatmeal, parsley, peas (dried), pilchards, rhubarb, rooibosch tea, rye, sardines, SESAME SEEDS, shrimps, sorghum, sorrel, soya beans, SPINACH, SPRATS, spring onions, sunflower seeds, watercress, wheatgerm, WHITEBAIT, wholemeal flour.

MAGNESIUM

Contributes to the utilisation of protein. Needed by the brain, nerves and muscles to enable them to relax and so is involved with the ability to sleep well. Improves muscle tone and is an important factor in the body's ability to purify itself.

Found in: Alfalfa, **ALMONDS,** apricots (dried), banana, BLACK TREACLE, bladderwrack, **BRAN (WHEAT), BRAZIL NUTS**, chick peas, cider vinegar, citrus fruits, **COCOA**, coconut, **COFFEE**, crab, **CURRY POWDER**, dandelion, dates, dulse, figs, **GINGER**, grouse, haricot beans, honey, kelp, kippers, MARMITE, milk powder, MOLASSES, MUNG BEAN SPROUTS, **MUSTARD**, okra pods, parmesan cheese, parsley, peaches (dried), PEANUTS, peppermint, raisins, rooibosch tea, rye, sardines, SHRIMPS, **SOYA BEANS**, spinach, sprats, sunflower seeds, sweet corn, tomato purée, WALNUTS, watercress, **WHEATGERM**, WHELKS, whitebait, WHOLEMEAL FLOUR, **WINKLES, YEAST (DRIED)**, yeast (fresh).

SILICON

Required for good eyesight and complexion, shiny hair, nerve efficiency, muscular tone and for good teeth enamel. Deficiency leads to baldness and is a contributory factor in skin, nervous and muscular diseases. A severe shortage of silicon has been implicated in a number of conditions including cancer, rheumatism, epilepsy and obesity. Horse-tail grass is probably the richest source of silicon in the world.

Found in: Alfalfa, artichokes, asparagus, barley, cabbage, celery, cider vinegar, comfrey, dandelion, leeks, mushrooms, oatmeal, radishes, spinach, strawberries, sunflower seeds, tomatoes, turnip.

FLUORINE (as Fluoride)

Deficiency leads to anaemia, headaches, skin troubles and poor teeth.

Found in: Broccoli cabbage, calabrese, cauliflower, cress, garlic, horseradish, kale, radish, seafood, spinach, spring greens, swede, tea, turnip, watercress.

PHOSPHORUS

Essential for brain, bones, lungs and nervous system and without it the glands do not function properly. Deficiency leads to poor memory, loss of vitality and muscular weakness – that 'always tired' feeling.

Found in: ALL FISH, MEAT, POULTRY AND GAME, ALMONDS, apricots (dried), asparagus, barley, **BRAN (WHEAT), BRAZIL NUTS**, broad beans, broccoli, BROWN RICE, brussel sprouts, buckwheat, butter beans, cabbage (raw), caraway seeds, carob, cashews, CHEESE, chick peas, cider vinegar, **COCOA**, coconut, COFFEE, comfrey, currants, CURRY POWDER, dates, EGG, **EGG YOLK**, endive, figs, GARLIC, haricot beans, HAZELNUTS, honey, horseradish, laverbread, lentils, LENTIL SPROUTS, liquorice root, maize (corn), marigold flowers, mayonnaise, milk (cows', goats', sheep's), **MILK POWDER**, millet, mung beans, MUNG BEAN SPROUTS, mushrooms, mustard and cress, OAT-MEAL, okra pods, parsley, parsnip, passion fruit, peaches (dried), PEANUTS, PEAS (DRIED), peas (fresh), PECANS, pepper, pistachio nuts, prunes, PUMPKIN SEEDS, raisins, RYE, salsify, sesame seeds, sorghum, sorrel, **SOYA BEANS**, spinach, sultanas, sunflower seeds, sweet corn, tomato purée, **WALNUTS**, watercress, **WHEATGERM**, WHOLEMEAL FLOUR, **YEAST (DRIED)**, YEAST (FRESH), yoghurt (live).

CHLORINE (as Chloride)

Deficiency causes toxins to build up in the body, poor digestion, loss of hair, muscle tone and sexual vitality.

Found in: Alfalfa, ALL WHITE FISH, **BACON, BAKED BEANS**, bananas, BARLEY, beef, beetroot, **BLACK TREA-CLE**, brazil nuts, **BUTTER**, carrots, CELERY, **CHEESE**, chick peas, cider vinegar, **COCOA**, COCONUT, **CRAB**, CURRY POWDER, DATES, EGGS, endive, fenugreek sprouts, FIGS,

FISH ROES, game, GOATS' MILK, KIDNEY, lamb, **LAVER-BREAD**, lentil sprouts, lettuce, LIVER, **LOBSTER, LOW FAT SPREAD, MARGARINE, MARMITE, MAYONNAISE**, milk (cows'), **MILK POWDER, MOLASSES**, mung beans, MUSHROOMS, mustard and cress, oatmeal, **OLIVES, OYSTERS**, PARSLEY, **PEANUT BUTTER**, pomegranate, pork, PORRIDGE OATS, poultry, rhubarb, **SARDINES**, sesame seeds, **SHRIMPS, SMOKED FISH**, spinach, sweet potatoes, tomatoes, turnip, VEAL, WATERCRESS, WHEATGERM, **WHOLEMEAL BREAD**, YOGHURT (LIVE).

SODIUM

Necessary for keeping calcium in solution. Deficiency results in cramp, slow-to-heal cuts and constipation. Excess leads to ulcers.

Found in: Alfalfa, All-Bran, **BACON**, baked beans, butter, canned vegetables, carrageen, carrots, celery, CHEESE, chick peas, chives, cider vinegar, cocoa, cod, crab, eggs, fennel, golden syrup, goose, HAM, honey, kidney, lamb, laverbread, lentils, lobster, low fat spread, margarine, **MARMITE**, nettles, oatmeal, okra pods, olives (stuffed), OX TONGUE, oysters, **PICKLES**, pork, porridge oats, **PRAWNS**, raisins, SALTED NUTS, sardines, scampi, sesame seeds, **SHRIMPS, SMOKED FISH**, sorrel, spinach, **STOCK CUBES**, strawberries, TOMATO KETCHUP, tuna, veal, watercress, **WINKLES**.

POTASSIUM

Needed to promote healthy heart, muscle and nerve tissue. Maintains balance of body fluids. Deficiency can lead to constipation, catarrh, gallstones and high blood pressure. Do not take salt if you have a potassium deficiency.

Found in: All fish, meat, poultry and game, alfalfa, ALMONDS, APRICOTS (DRIED), apricots (fresh), asparagus, avocado pear, baked beans, banana, barley, beetroot, blackberries, blackcurrants, **BLACK TREACLE**, borage, **BRAN (WHEAT)**, BRAZIL NUTS, broad beans, broccoli, brown rice, brussel sprouts, butter beans, cabbage, canteloupe melon, carrageen, carrot, **CAPSICUM (SWEET PEPPER)**, cashews, cauliflower, celeriac, celery, chamomile flowers, cheese, cherries, chick peas, chicory, cider vinegar, **COCOA**, coconut, **COFFEE**, comfrey, cucumber, currants, **CURRY POWDER**, damsons, dandelion, DATES, eggs, endive, fennel, **FIGS**, French beans, GARLIC, GINGER, globe artichoke, goose, gooseberries, grapefruit, grapes, greengages, grouse, haricot beans, hazelnuts, honey, HORSERADISH, Jerusalem artichokes, laverbread, leeks, lentils, LENTIL SPROUTS, lettuce, loganberries, maize (corn), **MARMITE**, milk (cows', goats', sheep's), MILK POWDER, millet, mint, MOLASSES, mulberries, mung beans, MUNG BEAN SPROUTS, mushrooms, MUSTARD, mustard and cress, nectarines, nettles, oatmeal, oranges, papaya, PARSLEY, parsnip, passion fruit, peaches, **PEACHES (DRIED)**, PEANUTS, peas (fresh and dried), pecans, peppermint, pineapple, pistachio nuts, plantain, pomegranate, potato, PRUNES, pumpkin, radishes, RAISINS, raspberries, red currants, rhubarb, rooibosch tea, runner beans, rye, salsify, sesame, sorghum, **SOYA BEANS**, spinach, spring onions, sultanas, summer savory, SUNFLOWER SEEDS, SWEET CHESTNUTS, sweet corn, sweet potato, tomato, **TOMATO PURÉE**, turnip, WALNUTS, WATERCRESS, **WHEATGERM**, wholemeal flour, yam, **YEAST (DRIED)**, YEAST (FRESH), yoghurt (live).

IRON

A constituent of haemoglobin, which carries oxygen round the bloodstream. Deficiency contributes to lack of muscle tone and general weakness, poor metabolism, anaemia and coldness of hands and feet.

Found in: Aduki beans, alfalfa, all meat and wild game, ALMONDS, APRICOTS (DRIED), arrowroot, ASPARAGUS PEA/BEAN, avocado pear, barley, blackcurrants, BLACK-EYED PEA, **BLACK TREACLE, BRAN (WHEAT)**, brazil nuts, BROAD BEANS, broccoli, brown rice, BUCKWHEAT, cashews, chick pea, cider vinegar, **COCKLES, COCOA**, coconut, COFFEE, comfrey, cranberries, **CURRY POWDER**, dandelion, dates, EGG, EGG YOLK, endive, figs, **GINGER**, haricot beans, hazelnuts, honey, horseradish, laverbread, liver, maize (corn), Marmite, MILLET, **MOLASSES**, mung beans, MUNG BEAN SPROUTS, mushrooms, MUSSELS, **MUSTARD**, mustard and cress, nettles, **OAT BRAN & OAT GERM**, OATMEAL, okra pods, olives, PARSLEY, passion fruit, PEACHES (DRIED), peanuts, peas, **PEPPER**, pilchards, pistachio nuts, prunes, PUMPKIN SEEDS, radishes, raisins, raspberries, RED KIDNEY BEANS, rooibosch tea, rye, salsify, sardines, scallops, sesame seeds, SORGHUM, SOYA BEANS, spinach, SPRATS, spring onions, spring greens, strawberries, sultanas, SUNFLOWER SEEDS, TOMATO PURÉE, turnip tops, walnuts, watercress, **WHEATGERM**, WHELKS, WHOLEMEAL FLOUR, WILD RICE, **WINKLES, YEAST (DRIED)**, YEAST (FRESH).

SELENIUM

Essential for normal liver function and white blood cell activity. A deficiency can cause high blood pressure and heart trouble.

Found in: Brewer's yeast, brown rice, eggs, fish, garlic, liver, wholemeal flour.

MANGANESE

A brain and nerve tonic, and is needed by the pituitary gland. Acts as an antiseptic and germicide. A growth factor in bone development. Deficiency can lead to arthritis.

Found in: Almonds, apricots, comfrey, dates, endive, honey, mint, nasturtium flowers, **OAT BRAN & OAT GERM**, olives, parsley, peanuts, potatoes, raisins, rooibosch tea, soya beans, tea, walnuts, watercress, wheatgerm.

IODINE

Regulates the thyroid gland. Helps the body to resist disease and lowers nervous tension. Excessive iodine is toxic.

Found in: Agar, artichokes, bladderwrack, carrageen, dulse, fish liver oils, garlic, Icelandic moss, Irish moss, kelp, laverbread, mushrooms, runner beans, seafood.

INDEX

This index indicates those recipes suitable for certain special or restricted diets by the use of the following symbols in the left-hand column: C suitable for a Candida Albicans Control Diet or a Yeast-free Diet; E suitable for an Egg-free Diet; G1 suitable for a Gluten-free Diet; Gr suitable for a Grain-free Diet; V suitable for a Vegan Diet. Any special restrictions or modifications needed to use these recipes when following one of these diets are given in the right-hand column and are preceded by the relevant symbol.

Note for Candida Albicans Control Diet: Foods excluded on this diet are as follows:- sugar, honey, fructose, glucose, malt, maple sugar, maple syrup, black treacle, molasses, date palm sugar, fruit, fruit juice (except lemon which is allowed in moderation), dried fruit, mushrooms, yeast, yeast extract, vinegar, dairy products, tamari (wheat-free soy sauce), peanuts, refined flours and starches. Yoghurt should also be avoided when Acidophilus is being taken, and has therefore been excluded from the recipes. Olive Oil is extremely beneficial for controlling Candida Albicans and should, therefore, be used instead of margarine or other oils whenever possible. It is inadvisable to follow this diet without medical supervision as careful supplementation is needed to avoid deficiencies of essential minerals and vitamins.

Bread: 22–34
  Amaranth Bread E, Gl, Gr, V 26   Gr use potato flour
  Banana Batter Bread Gl, Gr 34
  Brown Rice Batter Bread C, Gl 34   C use unsweetened soya milk
  Buckwheat and Rice Bread E, Gl, V 26
  Chick Pea Bread E, Gl, Gr, V 29
  Date and Walnut Loaf E, Gl, Gr, V 32   V use soya milk
  German Rye Bread E, V 23
  Gluten-free Breads 24–30, 32–4
  Maizemeal Bread C, Gl 33   C use unsweetened soya milk
  Malt Loaf E, V 31   E use Foodwatch whole egg replacer
                                      V use soya milk and Foodwatch whole
                                        egg replacer

  Millet Batter Bread C, Gl 33   C use unsweetened soya milk
  Millet Bread C, Gl 30   C omit honey
  Millet Fruit Loaf E, Gl, V 32
  Mixed Flour Bread E, Gl, V 28
  Potato and Buckwheat Bread E, Gl, Gr, V 25
  Potato and Chestnut Bread E, Gl, Gr, V 25
  Potato and Rice Bread E, Gl, V 25
  Potato and Soya Bread Gl, Gr 26
  Potato Soda Bread Gl, Gr 27
  Potato Soda Bread (egg-free) E, Gl, Gr, V 27
  Raisin Bread E, Gl, V 29
  Rice and Chestnut Bread E, Gl, V 26
  Rice, Soya and Raisin Bread Gl 30
  Rye Soda Bread C, E, V 23   C & V use water to mix
  Sorghum Batter Bread C, Gl 34   C use unsweetened soya milk
  Sorghum Bread C, Gl 30   C omit honey
  Sultana Bread E, Gl, V 29
  Traditional Rye Bread E, V 22
  Welsh Barley Bread E, V 24   V omit honey
Breakfast Biscuits V 48   V use soya or nut milk

Breakfast Cereals: 15–21
  Apricot Cereal E, Gl, Gr, V 19   Gl use millet or buckwheat flakes
                                      Gr use buckwheat flakes
  Brown Rice Porridge C, E, Gl, V 18   C serve with unsweetened soya or nut milk
                                      V serve with soya or nut milk
  Buckwheat Porridge C, E, Gl, Gr, V 15 C serve with unsweetened soya or nut
                                      milk
                                      V serve with soya or nut milk and omit
                                      honey
  Fresh Fruit Cereal E, V 20
  Millet Porridge C, E, Gl, V 17   C for variation (iii) use water or
                                      unsweetened soya milk
  Oatmeal Porridge C, E, V 18
  Polenta (Maizemeal Porridge) C, E, Gl, V 16 C serve with unsweetened soya or nut
                                        milk
                                      V serve with soya or nut milk
  Popcorn C, E, Gl, V 18   C omit honey
                                      V omit honey

Fruit Jelly **E, Gl, Gr, V** 95
Fruit Mousse **Gl, Gr** 96
Fruit Topped Cheesecake **Gl, Gr** 93   **Gl** use gluten-free biscuits of choice
                                           Gr use grain-free biscuits of choice

Golden Layer Dessert **Gl** 105
Grape Dessert **E, Gl, Gr, V** 101
Hawaiian Pineapple **E, Gl, Gr** 94
Ice-Cream Type Desserts **Gl, Gr** 99   **Gl** except coffee substitute variation
                                           Gr except coffee substitute variation
                                           V use agar agar
Mandarin Orange Jelly **E, Gl, Gr, V** 95
Milk Jelly **C, E, Gl, Gr, V** 96   **C** use unsweetened soya, nut or coconut
                                               milk and omit sweetener
                                           V use agar agar and soya or nut milk
Orange Jelly **E, Gl, Gr, V** 95   **V** use agar agar
Pashka **Gl, Gr** 94
Peacheesy Flan **Gl, Gr** 90   **Gl** use gluten-free pastry of choice
                                           Gr use grain-free pastry of choice

Pear and Millet Dessert **E, Gl** 102
Prune and Tofu Dessert **E, Gl, Gr, V** 103   **V** omit honey
Raspberry Sorbet **Gl, Gr** 100
Rhubarb and Ginger Whip **E, Gl, Gr** 103
Rum Almondeen **Gl, Gr,** 106   **Gr** use banana sponge cake
Spanish Cream **Gl, Gr** 97
Yoghurt and Apricot Flan **Gl, Gr** 90   **Gl** use gluten-free pastry of choice
                                           Gr use grain-free pastry of choice

Cold Savoury Dishes:
Carrot and Cheese Savoury **E, Gl, Gr** 143   **Gl** use millet or buckwheat flakes
                                                 Gr use buckwheat flakes
Haricot Bean Roast **C, E, Gl, Gr, V** 144   **C** use yeast-free breadcrumbs and omit
                                                    apple
                                                Gl use gluten-free breadcrumbs of
                                                    choice
                                                Gr use grain-free breadcrumbs of
                                                    choice
Haricot Bean 'Sausage Roll' Filling   **C** use yeast-free breadcrumbs and omit
C, E, Gl, Gr, V 144   apple
                                                Gl use gluten-free breadcrumbs of
                                                    choice
                                                Gr use grain-free breadcrumbs of
                                                    choice
Lentil Roast **C, E, Gl, Gr, V** 144   **C** use yeast-free breadcrumbs and
                                                    omit apple
                                                Gl use gluten-free breadcrumbs
                                                Gr use grain-free breadcrumbs of
                                                    choice
Lentil 'Sausage Roll' Filling **C, E, Gl, Gr, V** 144   **C** use yeast-free breadcrumbs and omit
                                                    apple
                                                Gl use gluten-free breadcrumbs of
                                                    choice
                                                Gr use grain-free breadcrumbs
                                                    of choice
Moulded Vegetable Salad **C, E, Gl, Gr, V** 161   **C** note special instructions for Aspic
                                                     V use agar agar

Gr use sago or tapioca milk pudding

V use soya milk and omit honey
V use soya milk and omit honey

C use yeast-free breadcrumbs and omit apple
Gl use gluten-free breadcrumbs of choice
Gr use grain-free breadcrumbs of choice

C use yeast-free breadcrumbs and omit apple
Gl use gluten-free breadcrumbs of choice
Gr use grain-free breadcrumbs of choice

C use yeast-free breadcrumbs and omit apple
Gl use gluten-free breadcrumbs of choice
Gr use grain-free breadcrumbs of choice

Gl use brown rice flour

C omit raisins

E use soya mayonnaise
C use soya mayonnaise
V use French Dressing

E except fried onion rings
C omit mushroom purée, sweet pickle, chutney and sugar
Gr use grain-free flour of choice

C use unsweetened soya milk and omit sugar

Gl use gluten-free pastry of choice
Gr use grain-free pastry of choice

C use lemon juice and olive oil in equal parts for dressing
V use French Dressing

C replace mushrooms with another vegetable

Gr use cider vinegar and tapioca flour

Gr use Potato and Chestnut Bread dough

C serve with unsweetened soya or nut milk

C omit honey
V omit honey

V use soya milk

Brown Rice Porridge C, E, Gl, V 18

Gl use diluted brown rice waffle batter
V use diluted egg-free or soya waffle batter made with brown rice flour

Brown Rice waffles C, E, Gl, V 40–2

C serve with unsweetened soya, nut or coconut milk
C use unsweetened soya, nut or coconut milk
E use egg-free or soya waffle batter made with brown rice flour
V use egg-free or soya waffle batter made with brown rice flour

Buckwheat and Rice Bread E, Gl, V 26
Carob Rice Biscuits Gl 55
Carob Sponge Cakes (Mud Huts) Gl 68
Chocolate Rice Biscuits Gl 55
Chocolate Sponge Cakes (Mud Huts) Gl 68
Coconut Brownies Gl 64
Coconut Cake Gl 76
Coconut Rice Fingers C, E, Gl, V 62

C use unsweetened soya, nut or coconut milk
E use Foodwatch whole egg replacer
V use Foodwatch whole egg replacer and soya milk

Creamed Rice Pudding E, Gl 115
Eggless Rock Cakes E, Gl, V 67
Eggless Sponge Cakes E, Gl, V 67
Fat-free Mini Sponges Gl 109
Flaked Rice and Tomato Soup C, E, Gl, V 128

C use unsweetened soya or nut milk
V use soya milk

Fruit and Nut Roly Poly Pudding Gl 108
Fruity Creamed Rice Pudding E, Gl 115
Fudge Cake Gl 73
Gingerbread E, Gl, V 80

E use Foodwatch whole egg replacer
V use Foodwatch whole egg replacer and soya milk
V omit honey

Ginger Nuts E, Gl, V 52
Gluten-free Florentines E, Gl, V 57
Honey and Hazelnut Cake Gl 76
Honey Tea Loaf Gl 81

Gl including variation (i) only

Japanese Rice Noodles 8
Millet and Rice Knobs C, E, Gl, V 39

C use unsweetened soya milk
V use soya milk

Mud Huts Gl 68
Noodle Soup C, E, Gl, V 127
Pineapple Upside-down Pudding Gl 107
Potato and Rice Bread E, Gl, V 25
Raisin 'N' Rice Pudding E, Gl 116
Rice and Buckwheat Crispbread E, Gl, V 47
Rice and Chestnut Bread E, Gl, V 26
Rice and Potato Pastry E, Gl, V 87
Rice and Sultana Buns Gl 65
Rice Flour Sponge Cake Gl 74
Rice Pastry E, Gl, V 86

C use yeast-free breadcrumbs and omit apple
Gl use gluten-free breadcrumbs of choice
Gr use grain-free breadcrumbs of choice

C use yeast-free breadcrumbs and omit apple
Gl use gluten-free breadcrumbs of choice
Gr use grain-free breadcrumbs of choice

C use yeast-free breadcrumbs and omit apple
Gl use gluten-free breadcrumbs of choice
Gr use grain-free breadcrumbs of choice

C use yeast-free breadcrumbs and omit apple
Gl use gluten-free breadcrumbs of choice
Gr use grain-free breadcrumbs of choice

C use yeast-free breadcrumbs and omit apple
Gl use gluten-free breadcrumbs of choice
Gr use grain-free breadcrumbs of choice

C use yeast-free breadcrumbs and omit apple
Gl use gluten-free breadcrumbs of choice
Gr use grain-free breadcrumbs of choice

Gr use banana flour sponge cake
Gr use arrowroot
V use maple syrup instead of honey

C omit gherkins

C use unsweetened soya milk and omit sweetener
V use soya milk

C use rye waffle batter made with unsweetened soya, nut or coconut milk
E use egg-free or soya waffle batter made with rye flour

V use egg-free or soya waffle batter made with rye flour

C use diluted rye waffle batter made with unsweetened soya, nut or coconut milk
E use diluted egg-free or soya waffle batter made with rye flour
V use diluted egg-free or soya waffle batter made with rye flour

C use unsweetened soya milk or water and omit sweetener
V use soya milk or water

C use water to mix
V use water to mix

C use unsweetened soya, nut or coconut milk
E use egg-free or soya waffle batter made with rye flour
V use egg-free or soya waffle batter made with rye flour

V use soya milk or water

Gr use cider vinegar

Gr use cider vinegar

V use cider vinegar

V use French Dressing
C omit apple
C use soya mayonnaise
V use French Dressing

C use soya mayonnaise
V use soya mayonnaise

C use soya mayonnaise

V use French Dressing or soya mayonnaise
V use silken tofu instead of yoghurt

C note special instructions for Aspic
V use agar agar
C use soya mayonnaise
E use soya mayonnaise
V use soya mayonnaise
Gr use cider vinegar
C omit gherkins

C use lemon juice and olive oil in equal parts for dressing
V use French Dressing
Gr use arrowroot

Gr use arrowroot
Gr use arrowroot
Gr use grain-free flour of choice
Gr use cider vinegar
Gr use arrowroot
V use maple syrup instead of honey
V use soya milk
V use soya milk

C use yeast-free breadcrumbs and omit apple
Gl use gluten-free breadcrumbs of choice
Gr use grain-free breadcrumbs of choice
C use yeast-free breadcrumbs and omit apple
Gl use gluten-free breadcrumbs of choice
Gr use grain-free breadcrumbs of choice
C use yeast-free breadcrumbs and omit apple
Gl use gluten-free breadcrumbs of choice
Gr use grain-free breadcrumbs of choice

Gl use millet or buckwheat flakes
Gr use buckwheat flakes

Gr use Soba (buckwheat spaghetti)
V use soya milk
C use lemon juice instead of vinegar
Gr use cider vinegar or lemon juice
V use agar agar

C use unsweetened soya milk and flavour with tomato instead of cheese or mushroom

C note special instructions for Aspic
V use agar agar
C note special instructions for Curry
Sauce

C omit cheese topping

Gl use chick pea flour
Gr use chick pea flour

Gr use arrowroot
Gr use arrowroot
Gl use gluten-free breadcrumbs of choice
Gr use grain-free breadcrumbs of choice
C replace mushrooms with another
vegetable

Gl use gluten-free pastry of choice
Gr use grain-free pastry of choice